I0825011

RESPELL
YOUR
REALiTY

LISA LISTER

RESPELL YOUR REALITY

The Art of Radical, Rhythmic (and Rebellious!) Self-Creation

RESPELL YOUR REALITY

The Art of Radical, Rhythmic (and Rebellious!) Self-Creation

Lisa Lister

First published in the UK and USA in 2026 by Watkins, an imprint of Watkins Media Limited, Unit 11, Shepperton House, 83–89 Shepperton Road, London N1 3DF

enquiries@watkinspublishing.com

Editorial Director: Ella Chappell
Managing Editor: Brittany Willis
Editorial Assistant: Caitlin Nolan
Head of Design: Karen Smith
Designer: Sarah O'Flaherty
Design Concept: Sneha Alexander
Production: Uzma Taj

A CIP record for this book is available from the British Library

ISBN: 978-1-78678-984-6 (Hardback)
ISBN: 978-1-83681-039-1 (eBook)

10 9 8 7 6 5 4 3 2 1

The manufacturer's authorised representative in the EU for product safety is:
eucomply OÜ - Pärnu mnt 139b-14, 11317 Tallinn, Estonia, hello@eucompliancepartner.com, www.eucompliancepartner.com

Typeset in Cera Pro & Esmeralda
Colour reproduction by Rival Colour
Printed in China

www.watkinspublishing.com

REWRITE THE RULES.

RECLAIM YOUR MAGIC.

CONJURE AND CULTIVATE A LIFE YOU LOVE.

CONTENTS

- Introduction 7
- **Part One: What Is Respelling Your Reality? 16**
  - You're the Architect of Your Reality 26
  - The Unprogramming 31
  - Self-Creation: The Recalibration 36
  - The Power of Your Rhythmic Intelligence 41
  - Rhythmic Creations, Rhythmic Realities 44
- **Part Two: The Creative Phases of the Moon 52**
  - New Moon: Dream. Imagine. Ideate. Vision. 54
  - Waxing Crescent Moon: Get Curious. Play. Be Fearless. 71
  - Waxing Quarter Moon: Disciplined Devotion 89
  - Waxing Gibbous Moon: Be Your Own Muse 106
  - Full Moon: Innovate. Be Seen. Express Yourself 123
  - Waning Gibbous Moon: Define. Refine. Align. Discern. 139
  - Waning Quarter Moon: Revelations. Revolutions. 156
  - Waning Crescent Moon: Reflect. Respect. Celebrate. 175
- **Part Three: Respell Your Reality for Life 190**
  - Create Your Own Respell Reality Map 192
  - Your Rhythmic (and Rebellious) Reality Respell 195
- Further Reading 204
- Big Love, All the Gratitude and Red Lipstick Kisses to . . . 207
- About the Author 208

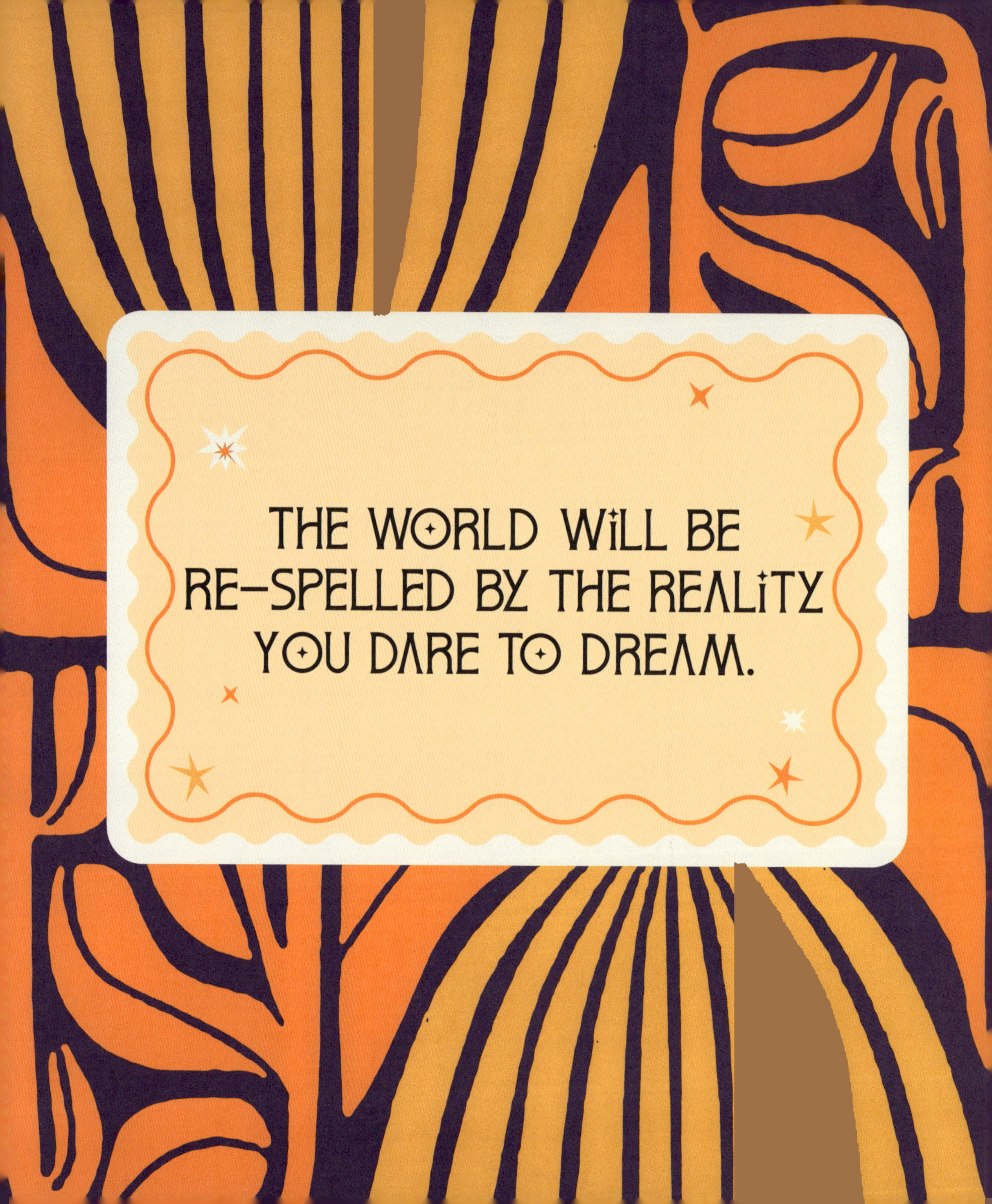
THE WORLD WILL BE
RE-SPELLED BY THE REALITY
YOU DARE TO DREAM.

INTRODUCTION

AS WE NAVIGATE THE SPACE BETWEEN WHAT'S BEEN BEFORE AND WHAT COMES NEXT, THESE IN-BETWEEN TIMES ARE CALLING THE ARTISTS, THE INTUITIVES, THE WITCHES, THE WOMEN WHO REMEMBER, THE REBELS, THE WISH-MIXERS, THE DREAMERS, THE ORACLES, THE CREATIVES, THE MULTIDIMENSIONAL THINKERS, THE MAGIC-MAKERS, THE VISIONARIES – YOU – TO CONJURE, CREATE AND CULTIVATE A NEW POSSIBILITY. A POSSIBILITY THAT WE CREATE. BECAUSE WE ARE MAGIC.

WE ARE THE CREATRIXES.

The current societal spell is strong. It has very successfully programmed many of us to believe that we're broken and need fixing; that how "good" we are is a defining metric of our value; that our creativity and power are superfluous and that we are somehow delusional if we choose to believe in magic.

Yet I know that because you're here and you've picked up this book, you understand that together we are stronger. That together we can and will *respell reality.*

Because reality is something that we get to dream, create, conjure, curate and direct.

We are the creatrixes of our reality, the mistresses of our magic, and we really do get to turn our dreams and vision for life into a work of art. We get to choose our own adventure and subvert the narrative, one storyline at a time. In fact, together we are the mother-loving plot twist this current timeline has been wanting, longing and waiting for.

If you feel like you've outgrown every self-help system you've ever loved, if you've tried manifesting, journaling, scripting, visualizing, pivoting, planning, and still wake up questioning just about everything, it's time to:

RESPELL YOUR REALITY

Respell Your Reality is a new and also ancient response. It's *not* another hustle-based life plan. It's *not* a rebranded productivity hack. It's a sensual, cyclical, creative self-creation experience – informed, directed and *spelled* by you – that's rooted in feminine rhythms, informed by quantum energetics and expressed through the marks, magic and moves that you make in the world. Yes, there is *some* science talk – not tons because that is *not* my jam – but I promise you won't need a lab coat. Just an open heart and a willingness to believe that what you *feel* can shape what becomes *real*.

It's a "rhythmic reality" designed to help you respell who you are, what (and how) you create and the life you live through the wisdom of your body, your cyclical intelligence and your creativity and imagination; because what I know for sure – as a woman, as a creative, as a human – is that we don't need more frameworks that pull us further away from our intuition and creative power. We need supportive structures that honour our cyclical, messy, magical, magnificent, glorious and luminous ways of the feminine.

RESPELL YOUR REALITY INVITES YOU TO FORGET THE RULES, TRENDS AND FORMULAS, AND REMEMBER YOUR MAGIC.

- **Your magic as an oracle and visionary and dreamer,** who can access ancient and future timelines and lifetimes to dream, define and refine the vision for your life and for these times.
- **Your magic as a cyclical creatrix,** who can sync your projects, plans and inner work to the natural rhythms of the Moon, your hormonal cycle and your energetic ebbs and flows; who can turn creative curiosity, dreams and wishes into shape and form to innovate and orchestrate your own experience and reality.
- **Your magic as a retelling, respelling, myth-making maven,** a multidimensional reality-bender who knows that every version of you lives on a timeline that you can choose to bring into form.

Yep, with your heart pointed in the direction of love and devotion, you can now stop waiting to "become" and start choosing who you already are – beneath the programming, the perfectionism and the people-pleasing – and commit to retelling and respelling, expressing, creating and sharing the storyline of *your* destiny. A life where you have the courage and self-power to express, create and really bloody live with your whole heart – which I believe (and we really do have to believe) can, and will, create ripples throughout the collective reality. *No. Big. Deal.*

This is the turning point. We have a choice. We can choose to consume more than we create and live a life where our thoughts, beliefs, creative expression and actions are dictated to us and pre-packaged by others. Or we can choose to return – radically, rhythmically and rebelliously – to what we innately know. My wildest hope is that we choose to return to the feminine-led, cyclical revolutions of our bodies, nature and the cosmos to support the creation of our inner and outer revolutions, living by our own rhythms and rituals, and respelling our reality.

Your Reality = Your Spell

What you believe, narrate, speak out loud and, most importantly, *live* becomes the world that you walk through and experience daily. The words you speak, the actions you take, the rituals you create are reality-makers. You can be walking side by side with someone and be experiencing a completely different reality to them because your frameworks, frequencies and stories simply don't match.

So, what *is* reality?

A consensus.

A construct.

A story.

A spell – one that *you* can rewrite and retell because you're in it and you can shape it. And if someone tells you otherwise . . . well, maybe that's *their* reality, not yours. Just saying.

Be Your Own Biggest Fan

Let's be clear, while the term "love yourself" has been heavily hijacked, it really is the script-flip that's absolutely and positively needed if we're to respell our reality, reclaim our creative power and, well, *create*. Loving ourselves, trusting ourselves, accepting ourselves and backing ourselves is what will activate our capacity to remember and, more importantly, *mistress* our magic. And I know this may seem super-conceptual and not at all practical, especially if we're tired/fretful/busy being a mumma to our family/trying to make money – I get it, but please hear me out . . .

I've been an author, storyteller, artist, creatrix of words, experience and art, and, more specifically, a conscious respeller of my own reality for over 20 years now. I'm a woman from a lineage of traveller women, witches and wise ones, who very much knew and know the magical capacity of women to dream and create entire realities into being. Now, remembering my magic and power as a creatrix has never really been the problem for me, but holding it and sustaining it? That has definitely been . . . trickier. (*Total. Bloody. Understatement.*) So, how in a world that wants us to conform and comply, can we all make art, express ourselves and create an authentic life where we're thriving, and where our reality is one that we've spelled? Well, it requires mistress-ry. As an artist, a writer, a lover, a live-er of life, I learned how to mistress my magic through trusting and believing in my connectivity to something that supports my magic and creative power.

Now, many of us who consider ourselves rebels, artists and visionaries reject the idea of structure, thinking that our creativity, passion and ideas will somehow be tamed and restrained by it; and while that can definitely be true, especially if you're trying to create in the goal-serving mechanism of the over-culture . . . there is another way.

Rhythms and Rituals

That way is the cyclical consistency of ebb and flow, expansion and contraction, the inhale and exhale, descent and ascent, the light and dark of our rhythmic intelligence. It's the ancient wisdom and knowing, realized and ritualized, that provides strong roots which will allow you to remember who you are beyond the realms of convention (i.e., all that you're told to believe) – which is somebody who is an oracle, a creatrix, a shapeshifter of realities, someone who can be a magnetic maven and an energetic match for a life worth living, a life defined and created by *you*.

This book uses the eight phases of the Moon to highlight and illustrate power phases for flow, magnetism and ideation, phases for life edits and evaluation, and phases to rest and digest, which will support you in tracking and mapping, exploring, conjuring and curating your own creative power. It's a monthly evolution, (which can also be mapped onto the menstrual cycle), and a new way of living, a sacred and creative rhythm that can reshape your identity, your projects, your path.

This isn't a prescribed plan or formula; it's a process that will support you in discovering who you *really* are – without apologies, endless disclaimers and the need to people-please – so that you are sourced – whole, lit up, connected to and rooted in divine original, creative and in-your-power feminine intelligence, satiated and strengthened, able to hold and mistress your magic and create your own reality.

And it *will* bring up "stuff". That's the idea. It will highlight the fears, the blocks, the shadows – the concerns about being seen, the worries about being raw and vulnerable, censored and cancelled – and for those of us who have been burned, silenced and persecuted for telling our truth in past lives, it may also bring up the question, "Why would I go and do that again?!" Which is why you don't have to do this work alone . . .

Meet Your Moon Mavens

Make no mistake, it's a bold and radical move to track and chart and really feel, then follow your heart's true path, to subvert, shape and spell your reality. While the most powerful muse is and always will be yourself, there are creatives and visionaries who have gone before us who hold *big* magic as cheerleaders, supporters and way-showers. I'll be sharing mine – mavens who have been a force and source of remembrance; women who had a lust for life, for colour, for vitality; women who dreamed ideas and entire worlds into being and put themselves in amongst it, who dared to do it differently and who can and will act as guides in each Moon phase. You'll be guided by the ebb and flow of the Moon *and* a circle of creative women who curated their lives as living spells; who dared, dreamed and declared their desires and shaped and spelled their own realities.

I repeat, these women are *not* muses; they're not perfect icons on a pedestal – far from it. In fact, if and when you go off and research/hang out with these women, you'll find that they're wild and messy; they made mistakes and they were magnificent makers of entire worlds. As you move through each Moon phase, they will offer you the chance to reflect, a spark of inspiration, a prompt to stir your creative fire.

Let them dare you to go further, to dig deeper, to create more boldly. This is not about you imitating or becoming them; it's about letting their stories, magic and experiences activate *your* stories, magic and experiences.

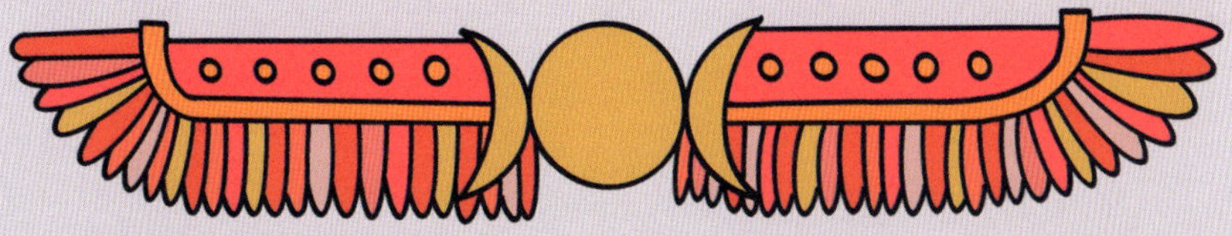

THE MOON MAVENS

New Moon – Niki de Saint Phalle: Dream it. Be bold. Sculpt your reality from your wildest desires.

Waxing Crescent Moon – Beatrice Wood: Play, flirt with possibility and follow your curiosity.

Waxing Quarter Moon – Octavia E. Butler: Commit to your creation with disciplined devotion.

Waxing Gibbous Moon – Frida Kahlo: Be your own muse, take yourself seriously and create your own reality.

Full Moon – Vali Myers: Live fully, love fiercely and express yourself in wild brilliance.

Waning Gibbous Moon – Madame Yevonde: Refine, align and define your creative direction.

Waning Quarter Moon – Amrita Sher-Gil: Revelations and revolutions. Let your truth be told.

Waning Crescent Moon – Faith Ringgold: Reflect, respect, celebrate your story and its power.

Regardless of whether you want to make art a daily practice, *Respell Your Reality* will help you to bring a creative project to fruition, revolutionize your relationships and/or embrace, share and express all aspects of yourself in the most real, true and authentic way. It will:

- Strengthen, satiate and most importantly sustain your capacity to remember, mistress and magnetize your magic and creative power.
- Ritualize and revere the rhythms of all things.
- Encourage/cheer-lead/butt-kick yourself into using your creative power to create entire worlds, write, paint and/or sing yourself into them and enchant a new spell.

Your life is not limited to one lunar cycle. Nor are you limited to one creation. Which is why this book is not a read-it-once-and-shelve-it situation; it's something that I've created for you to return to month after month, cycle after cycle, season after season, year after year, creation after creation. Because every time you step into a new Moon cycle, you'll connect with fresh desires, fresh energy and fresh layers, and your rhythms will reveal new and ancient wisdom as you experience and respell *your* reality.

Loves, it's time to get revolution-ready – to revive, ritualize and devote ourselves to the power of art, beauty, creativity and magic in each and every one of us; to meet the version of yourself – encoded in rhythm, waiting to be written – and to respell your reality.

I step into the creation of my life.
I am both the artist and the art.
I choose to create, shape and spell it.
My reality, respelled, my way.

PART ONE

WHAT iS RESPELLiNG YOUR REALiTY?

THE ART OF RESPELLING YOUR REALITY

SOME PEOPLE *MIGHT* CALL THIS MANIFESTING. IN THE REALMS OF STORYTELLING, IT *MIGHT* BE REFERRED TO AS WORLD-BUILDING, WHICH FEELS A LITTLE CLOSER TO HOW I EXPERIENCE IT (AND I'M A WRITER, SO THAT WOULD MAKE MORE SENSE); BUT TO ME, IT'S MOSTLY ABOUT REMEMBERING – BODY, BONE, CELL-DEEP REMEMBERING – THAT YOU AREN'T A PASSIVE PARTICIPANT IN YOUR LIFE AND THAT YOU HAVE THE ABILITY AND CAPABILITY TO CONSCIOUSLY CRAFT AND CREATE REALITY, RATHER THAN SIMPLY ACCEPT WHAT YOU'RE GIVEN.

I don't know about you, but I have zero interest in closing my eyes, crossing my fingers tight and hoping – really hard – that the universe drops all my dreams and wishes directly into my lap (although I did do that as a kid and sometimes it worked; it's how I learned to trust that it's possible, but it can become a very hit-or-miss process). No, to respell your reality, you have to move beyond wishful thinking and actively create it.

Why? Because, for the longest time, our reality has been written for us. Women especially have been written into stories that we didn't author, cast in roles we didn't audition for, and taught to adjust and conform, disconnecting us from our innate power to create, shape and originate. We've lived for far too long in a reality that's been designed for our obedience and not our brilliance, which is why we must remember and then reclaim our creative power and magic – and our capacity to shape and spell reality.

How? Look, there are a gazillion things I can and will share about the how (spoiler alert: this whole book is the how), but from my experience, the how – and this is a super-simplified version – is a three part-er (because three always has been, and always will be, the magic number).

1. **Start by witnessing the patterns and beliefs** that you've inherited from outside sources about how you "should" live and experience your life. Some of mine have included the beliefs that we must have kids (I haven't); get a "proper" job (By that, I guess they mean a safe and secure line of work that pays money at the same time every month – I've always done the weirdest and wildest things for work and, for the most part, had a lot of fun doing them!); and get married (I *did* do that, but that's because (a) my husband is a hot Viking and I want to spend a lot of time with him, (b) I love a party and (c) there is nothing conventional about our marriage – and that's why it works!).
2. **Then choose.** Choose to no longer accept familial, societal and cultural patterns and beliefs. Choose to actively retell and respell them in your own words, your own rhythm and your own true-to-you wildness. Some call this mindset work, but what I know from working with women and their cyclical nature for over 20 years is that our stories are in our bodies – the good, the bad and the glorious spectrum that sits between, including the stories from across lifetimes and timelines – and that no amount of "mindset work" will help the retelling and respelling of your reality if you don't feel safe in your body. This is why we work with the feminine rhythms and their keys and codes to know ourselves better, to remember our power and magic, and, more importantly, to trust ourselves and the decisions we make, so that you can . . .

3. **Spend the rest of your life crafting, curating, conjuring and creating** a life that might not necessarily be perfect (chances are, it won't be) and that may not necessarily be in alignment with familial, cultural and societal ideals and beliefs, but is absolutely and fully in line with yours.

Manifestation, as it's often taught, tells you to think positive thoughts, to visualize or to script a future, but it doesn't ask you to fully participate. It rarely invites you to get messy with your making, to actively energize and juice up your dream life, and to honour your cyclical nature – of building and burning, of birthing and resting, of tending to your desires – and to be in relationship with it *all* through your body and your sensorial nature.

It's the spell you cast, the vision you hold, the magnetic force that draws what you desire toward you, because real manifesting isn't passive – far from it – it's an act of deep and daily action and alignment to become a frequency match. You don't just wish and hope for something; you remember that it already exists and you lift and shift your energy, so that your physical self has no choice but to follow, and become the version of yourself who naturally magnetizes and calls it in.

Respelling your reality is different from manifesting 101 because:

- **It's creative.** You're not just thinking and dreaming about the life you want, although you are doing that . . . *and* you're actively shaping it – with your hands, heart, choices, rituals, words and art. You're not just dreaming about the woman who lives in Paris, writes saucy romance novels, takes lovers and wears red lipstick (wait, is that just me?). You're making choices from *her* perspective and breathing life into *her* existence. You don't hope for it; you remember it and you become it.
- **It's cyclical.** You're not expected to hold one truth, story, experience or vibrational frequency forever. (Thank the goddess for *that*!) You honour the natural rhythm of expansion, contraction and renewal.

You trust that you can rest without losing momentum and sustain the act of creation without burning out. It becomes the container in which the design, texture and colour of your life can come into being.

- **It's participatory.** You're not waiting to be chosen by the universe; you're co-creating with it, weaving your magic into the fabric of your everyday life through the aesthetics you choose, the rituals and rhythms that you honour and the tiny details that you pay attention to that make a dream feel real.
- **It's rebellious.** You're done playing by someone else's rules and refuse to outsource your power to external systems; and you design a life that isn't dictated by your circumstances. You strip away all the stories that told you who you *should* be, so you can stand fully in who you *are* – you choose your pace, your path and your pleasure, and you trust your body and your cyclical nature as guides. Except, most people live inside a reality that they didn't consciously create.

At some point, we've all been convinced that life was something that happened to us – that the script has already been written, the roles in our life have already been cast, and that our "job" is just to play along and adjust accordingly to the set pieces that have been handed to us. We've taken the script that's been written and crafted by our family, friends, society, culture and the media we consume, and we simply recite the lines.

And specifically as women, our reality is often shaped and formed in response to systems and structures that are not, and never have been, designed in our favour. Now, what I will say is that we've become wildly skilled, Olympic-athlete-level proficient at adapting and surviving – but it's this that's making so many of us anxious, tired and burned out. That's the idea. They want us so bloody exhausted that we forget our magic and creative power – and yet it's our magic and creative power that have made us so bloody good at performing a curated-for-the-over-culture personality.

Common Survival Strategies

Here's some of the most common, often unconscious ways we've learned to perform, adapt and survive (our magic and creative power in action):

Fitting In versus Shape-Shifting

Becoming what's expected. Dressing "appropriately". Knowing when to be smaller and blending in to avoid threat. This is a lifelong performance that many of us learn from a very young age.

Survival skill: adaptability
Shadow cost: disconnection from our real and true self

People-Pleasing versus Harmonization

Keeping the peace. Avoiding conflict. Being likeable. Many of us are conditioned to prioritize the comfort of others, especially men's, at the expense of our own boundaries and needs.

Survival skill: social intuition
Shadow cost: self-erasure

Hyper-Vigilance versus Intuition

Scanning the room. Reading the mood. Anticipating threat. Many of us are experts at sensing what's unspoken, an informed-by-trauma radar that we develop for our physical or emotional safety.

Survival skill: intuition
Shadow cost: anxiety, adrenal fatigue

Self-Surveillance versus Knowing Yourself

Monitoring your body, tone, weight, voice, ambition. Under the influence of the over-culture, we've learned to watch ourselves through the gaze of others.

Survival skill: social compliance
Shadow cost: chronic self-doubt, dysmorphia, disempowerment

Over-Functioning versus Multi-Tasking

Women often learn to be twice as competent to be considered half as worthy. That means saying yes to everything, taking on emotional labour, perfectionism, and being seen and known as the "reliable one".

Survival skill: capacity to experience many things
Shadow cost: burnout, resentment, invisibility

Armouring Up versus Protection and Discernment

Growing a thick skin. Detaching from softness, sensuality and emotion to succeed in male-dominated environments. This can look like being hyper-independent/rejecting anything deemed "too feminine".

Survival skill: self-protection
Shadow cost: emotional suppression, isolation

Knowledge Hoarding versus Curiosity

Becoming experts. Gaining degrees. Reading the room and reading the books. Because we've been taught that we need credentials and evidence to be believed, even about our own experiences.

Survival skill: mastery
Shadow cost: impostor syndrome

Living in Duality versus Mutability

Being both nurturing and assertive, sexy but not "too much"; ambitious but modest. This dance is exhausting and often invisible. But women master it, daily.

Survival skill: fluidity
Shadow cost: fragmentation, exhaustion

This list isn't exhaustive, and not every woman will relate to all of it, and it's a perfect illustration of how our own magic and creative power have been distorted to create habits that are rooted in the wisdom of survival. This has never been more visible than in the act and art of performing.

The Feminine Art of Performance

Performing for the patriarchy is about external validation. It's shaped by how we believe we'll be perceived, desired and/or consumed. It's often unconscious, habitual and woven in to how we move, speak, dress and present ourselves, even how we show up on social media, because we've been taught from such a young age that our value lies in how desirable and how pleasing we are.

The *art* of performance, as it was practised in ancient feminine traditions? Now, that's an entirely different frequency.

It was never about being watched; it was all about invoking. It was performance as the most sensual and sacred spellwork and embodiment – a way of channelling the divine *through* the body. Think of the temple dancers in India, the priestesses of Isis in Egypt, the Delphic Oracle in Greece, the Vestal Virgins in Rome, the courtesans who were poets and artists as well as lovers. These weren't performers in the modern sense: they were vessels, transmitters, bridges between the worlds.

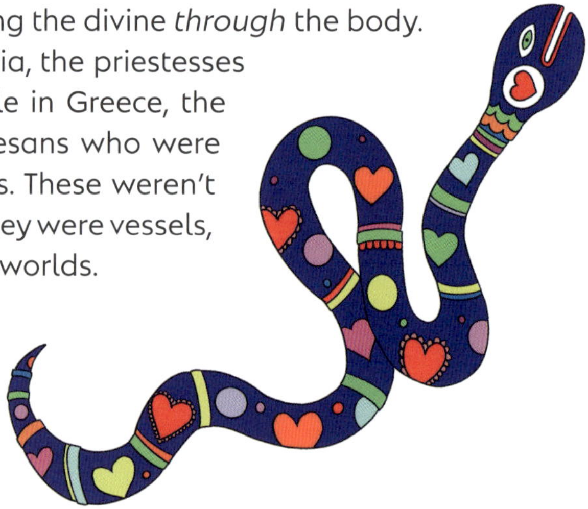

These women were performing to commune and their movement, music, voices and rituals weren't meant to seduce in the contemporary way that we understand seduction; it was meant to open portals. They performed to honour the divine, to enact myth, to initiate others, to embody the mysteries and to remember. Performance was power. It was ecstatic. It was medicinal. It was the feminine in her fullest agency, demanding attention, not submitting to it. The performance itself was a form of knowledge transmission; it was a spiritual technology all of its own.

So, the real difference is this: one performance is done to be seen in a way that pleases others. The other is done to reveal what cannot be spoken in words. One depletes; the other channels. One is passive; the other is intentional. One collapses the self into a curated projection; the other expands the self into an archetype, a ritual, a self-created mythos, a force of mother-loving nature.

And now many of us (which is why I'm writing this book and why you're reading it) are remembering this and we're realizing that it's time to call back, reclaim and revere our magic and creative power – All. Of. It. – and move from survival mode to creating new realities.

We now know (and if you don't remember that you know yet, you will – wink) that reality isn't fixed. It's fluid, malleable and shape-able. We now know that we are future-femme-coded – not bound by past narratives of what femininity is supposed to be, but instead, we're creating our own version of feminine power, rooted in both ancient wisdom and radical possibility. What's Been Before wasn't able to make meaning of, or metabolize what it is that we are here for and capable of; and as we witness the end of an era that simply couldn't/wouldn't receive you and your magic and creative power, the question isn't (and never has been) whether you can create and respell reality, it's whether you dare to. Well, do you?

YOU'RE THE ARCHITECT OF YOUR REALITY

(AND YOU ALWAYS HAVE BEEN)

YOU ARE THE CREATRIX. YOU ALWAYS HAVE BEEN. THE WORLD YOU CURRENTLY LIVE IN AND EXPERIENCE ON THE DAILY? IT'S ONE THAT YOU'VE UNCONSCIOUSLY BEEN BUILDING AND CURATING ALL ALONG. NOW IT'S TIME TO DO IT CONSCIOUSLY. WITH INTENTION. (AND A *LOT* OF DEVOTION.)

Respelling your reality is the conscious act of remembering, choosing and deciding who you are beyond conditioning, beyond survival mode and beyond the stories you've inherited. This isn't simply about attracting and/or building a "future" life; it's about knowing *that* life already exists and that you are the woman who chooses to align with, and match, the frequency of that version of herself who is already living and experiencing it (and really bloody loving it too)!

If you've been conditioned to shrink, to take up less space, to adjust to the worlds of others rather than create your own, that ends now. What we're doing here is feminine-centred world-building – our future is femme-coded – and the woman who knows she is the architect of her own reality?

She's unstoppable.
She's magnetic.
She's power-full.
She's *you*.
So tell me, what reality are *you* respelling?

Where to Start

A favourite maven of mine is French–American author, diary-keeper, myth-maker and high priestess of personal truth Anaïs Nin. Anaïs is *exactly* how I like my women best – controversial, contradictory and complicated – and if she were alive today, I guarantee she would have been "cancelled" ten times over. *At least.* Except, she was never trying to be a moral compass – far bloody from it, ha!

She believed that individuals have to create our own worlds, because the world presented to us is simply "not sufficient" – *yes*, Anaïs! In fact, she believed that writing and art allowed for the creation of a "personal reality".

She dared to share her creation of "personal identity", and in it we meet the self that isn't always likeable; the self that dares to desire "too much"; and the self that contradicts, changes her mind, yearns, betrays, imagines. The self that refuses to be shaped into, and by, simplicity. She is proof – to me at least – that even if we are messy, controversial, misunderstood, it's *all valid*.

When you respell your reality, you develop what some call a "self-concept" and what Anaïs called a "woman's point of view", which is, essentially, a unique-to-you (and definitely *not* created to appease and please the male gaze) way in which to create and experience yourself and your reality. It's about unlearning and deprogramming yourself from the stories you've inherited that are absolutely not yours.

There's a chance that people have projected their views and opinions onto you so much that you're no longer aware or sure exactly who you are, what you believe in and what is real and true to you. This might mean that you don't really recognize yourself anymore when you look in the mirror, as you've become a pleasing version of yourself that suits everyone else, but which is absolutely not a true representation of you and all that you are. It's a bit like wearing a cheap faux-fur coat bought from a charity shop: at first glance it may look OK, but it doesn't actually fit, it's uncomfortable to wear for long periods of time and, let's face it, it goes with absolutely nothing that you own.

I believed for a really long time that I had to suffer to earn success – an old story that kept me trapped in a no-fun loop. What I know now that I didn't then, is that there are infinite realms of possibility available to us in every moment, and all are based on the state that we choose to experience. When I chose to stop believing the story that I had to suffer (which definitely took some doing) and found that ritualized repetition can outsmart those versions of myself that didn't want to let go of that idea, and that instead I could let success – or my idea of it at least – be easy, my reality adjusted.

Respelling your reality is about reconnecting with your senses and emotions. Many of us have learned to survive in a reality that hasn't been set up to support us, which has meant we've become disconnected from our bodies, our cyclical nature and our felt experience; and yet it's our sensorial nature that holds some of the major keys and codes to what we really want, need and desire. Again, this is a biggie, as many of us have got so good at performing for others, we have no idea what it is that we actually want, need and desire. For me, reconnection to the sensorial self – the body, the cycles, the felt experience

– looks and feels like savouring everything; tracking my cyclical nature and noticing how my energy, emotions and libido shift according to the Moon and my menstrual cycle; and spending more time than not without a bra, a filter or a plan.

It's about using your voice in uncensored expression, whether that's speaking out loud, singing, chanting or sighing even. I'm married to a dude who makes no apologies for breathing, speaking while eating and expressing himself. LOUDLY. I, on the other hand, noticed early on in our relationship that I rarely, if ever, breathe audibly. Turns out it's something I learned from a very early age to "contain", so that I was seen and not heard – well, you'd best believe I do everything (and I mean *everything*) out loud now!

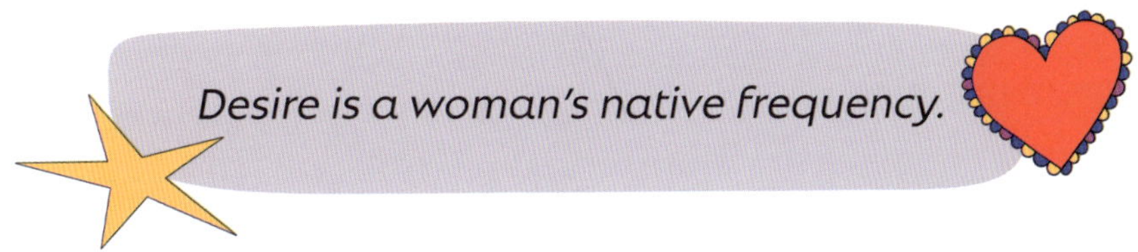

Respelling your reality is about you claiming your desires without apology, but for the reasons we've already outlined, we rarely, if ever, lead with and live from our desires. We've been taught – really bloody well – to keep our desires (if we can even name them) under wraps, so we live from duty, fear or survival. It can be terrifying to claim your desires and live from them, because real desire doesn't always sound "reasonable". It rarely fits the identity that you've worked carefully to maintain, and because it's usually a part of you that's previously been tamed and ignored, there's a big chance that it's hungry. Ravenous, even. And it will most definitely want more . . .

Which is why I am a big fan of daily devotionals. I share about them in my book *Self Source-ery*. They are daily rituals and practices that encourage us to follow our excitement, curiosity and eagerness in every moment toward what feels most alive. Let curiosity, not control, lead the way.

This is about you being full of yourself. I know that for many of us the idea of being full of ourselves will equate to being "too much". Many of us would have been told, "Oh, she's so full of herself", like that's a *bad thing*. I mean, and I say this often, who else are you going to be bloody full of? Hopefully not everyone else's versions of you, that's for sure, and yet society would rather that than you becoming *more* of yourself and filling yourself all the way up with your magic. With the things that *you* love, want, need, desire. With *your* medicine. With care. With nourishment. Yet this has been called, and sadly probably will still be considered by some, to be a selfish act.

Personally? What I think is *really bloody selfish* is to abandon and betray ourselves simply to please and appease others. So ditch *all* the versions of yourself that have been given and/or that have been projected on to you, and get really OK with being *full of yourself*.

Respelling your reality is you witnessing, and being witnessed, in spaces that celebrate complexity and contradiction. We are *not* linear, nor is reality, and the more we get comfortable with that – with knowing that there isn't necessarily one "right" truth – the more we can let ourselves be messy in exploring our personal truth (which is a truth that will look, feel, sound and be different to someone else's personal truth – and that's OK). When we get familiar and come into relationship with our personal truth, this makes it much easier to trust that our way of seeing, experiencing and creating the world is valuable, essential, valid and beautiful.

What you know to be true about yourself, based on what you think, feel and expect, becomes your lived experience – it's the law of quantum physics – so through deliberate and devotional self-creation, you become more real than you've ever dared to be. You sync to a deeper, older, ancient drumbeat of feminine knowing, while retelling and respelling entirely new realities. It's science *and* it's magic.

THE UNPROGRAMMING

THE EXPERIENCE OF "BEING FULL OF YOURSELF" IS UNCOMFORTABLE, BECAUSE IT MEANS YOU'LL OFTEN BE MOVING IN A DIFFERENT DIRECTION TO MOST OF THE CURRENT DOMINANT CULTURE, AND THAT CAN PROVOKE THOSE WHO REMAIN UNDER THE SOCIETAL SPELL – SO THERE IS NO JUDGEMENT OF THOSE WHO *DO* CHOOSE TO STAY THERE.

I've written on numerous occasions over the past 20 years about how there's definitely a part of me that would like to put back the onion layers I've pulled back and *not know* what I now know, or feel what I feel or see what I see . . . and yet I also know that's *not* my path. I realize that so many of us have experienced that if/when we *do* choose ourselves, it's at the risk of potentially disappointing others and/or receiving heat for it. For example, I don't go out of my way to do things differently and provoke others, but I know that sometimes I'm the sand in someone's knickers, not by saying or doing anything wildly controversial, but simply by showing up, as me.

The actress Mae West is my guiding force in this forever practice. She knew who she was and what she wanted, and she went right ahead and got it. At the age of 40, she became a breakout star, in a world that already wanted to retire her to the shadows.

She wrote her own lines. Literally. She wrote the plays that made her famous, including *Sex* (banned for "corrupting the morals of youth") and *The Drag* (one of the first plays to spotlight gay life with empathy and heat).

When the studio execs tried to tame her, she'd hand them a script that she'd already written and edited.

Mae is the epitome of being full of yourself. She defied all of the projections of who she *should* be (according to others) and was so full of herself that she was unshakable. My biggest take-away from Mae is that as long as you know who the fuck you are, what you're about, what you stand for, what fills you up – then everything else? It's just noise.

I've often (far too many mother-loving times) let the opinions others have of me, and even worse, the perceived opinions that I think they'll have of me, stop me from being my full self. Yet, my relationship with my rhythmic and cyclical nature, with self-creation and the respelling of my reality – me on my own terms – means that my one "job" is to ask myself: "What makes me feel most alive?", and to choose that. Every. Single. Time.

Because the other option? It's really fucking miserable. Betraying and abandoning yourself to be a likeable and tame version of yourself? I'm no longer available for that option. Ever.

So, defiantly – because you know that the phrase "you're full of yourself" is one that's often used in a derogatory and disapproving way, usually toward a woman, and intended to keep us disconnected from our power – respell your reality and let yourself be full.

Meet your needs.
Satiate your hunger.
Be full. Of yourself.
Be full of your power.
Your pleasure.
Your truth.
Your magic.

This is what authenticity looks and feels like to me, and I share that because, while I'm aware that the term "authenticity" has potentially become overused and lost its meaning, to really respell your reality in your most true-to-you authentic way, you will have to risk being misunderstood by others in order to finally understand yourself. Especially if you, and I really hope that you do, want to live from that place and space.

To live authentically, you'll be doing things that your old self never felt safe doing, such as saying no, claiming space, changing course, walking away, speaking up and standing out. You'll be letting go of your "good girl" conditioning and the ideas of spiritual "performance" (when someone is fluent in the *look* of devotion – the clothes, the crystals, the yoga-teacher softly spoken voice – but there's no roots, no mess, no mystery. It's not that beauty, ritual or aesthetics are wrong – I personally love them. It's when those things are hollow, or are replacing spiritual depth, that it becomes "performance"), hustle as worthiness, productivity as proof, perfect image as protection . . . the list is endless.

Get Safe in Your Self

Your body needs to know it's safe to be *that* woman. Now, I can't promise it'll ever truly be "safe" to be a woman who is full of herself and led by her desires and what lights her all the way up – no permission slips required; I've not got any proof of that in this world (which is why I'm always looking to and sharing in reverence the stories of the women who have been before us), because what I *do* know, for absolute certain, is that without nervous system support, it can and will feel like a threat.

AN IN.YOUR.BODY.MENT TOOLKIT

Some nervous system support tools from my own In.Your.Body. Ment medicine bag include:

- **Track your body's cues:** Become aware of the moves that your body makes and what they mean to you. Self-knowledge is self-power. There's absolutely no one-size-fits-all approach to this, but knowing when your shoulders are creeping up to your earlobes or your jaw is getting tight (and what those body cues are responding to and how they make you feel) will provide much-needed intel on how you and your body communicate.
- **Focus on your breath:** I find bringing my attention to my breath, with no judgement as to how deep or shallow it is, and giving myself a moment to soften into my body really helps.
- **Take a moment to yourself:** Pause before entering high-stakes conversations. Tapping your collarbones gently with your first two fingers and/or doing a little Taylor Swift-style full-body shake-out can also be really helpful.
- **Let pleasure guide you back into your body:** Use scent, music, soft fabrics, good food and/ or dance to bring you back to the present, to your body, to what matters.

- **Know when enough is enough:** Honour your capacity to know when to push your edge, and when to rest and regroup. (This takes practice, and you may not get it right every time, so don't berate yourself; you're simply witnessing when, "Oh, I could have gone a little further there," or, "Oops, I've gone too hard here, I definitely need to sit this one out."
- **Practise resourcing rituals:** Besides breath-work and putting your attention on your breath, these can include things like vagus nerve stimulation through the simple acts of humming or gargling water, old-school-style pen-and-paper journaling, or my personal favourite: lying on the floor or on the bed with your legs up the wall.

Look, while there is no pre-approved road map for choosing yourself over the system or becoming your own oracle and myth-maker, I do believe (and I'm aware this is a bold and audacious statement, but what can I say? I back myself!) that what I'm sharing here, in this book – through cyclical ancient/future wisdom – is a spell that we can all cast to unhook, unlearn, reimagine, reclaim and respell our realities. Not once. But again. And again. And with the fiercest love and devotion on repeat, so that we create and live a life that echoes our essence, a life where we are wildly alive.

SELF-CREATION

THE RECALIBRATION

WE LIVE IN A CULTURE THAT'S OBSESSED WITH SURFACE-LEVEL REINVENTION: THE GLOW-UPS, THE REBRANDS, THE "ELEVATED UPGRADE". IT'S RELENTLESS, SO THE IDEA OF SELF-CREATION MAY FEEL LIKE A SUPERFICIAL AND SUPERFLUOUS ACT, BUT REAL SELF-CREATION – THE KIND THAT REWRITES, RETELLS AND RESPELLS YOUR ENTIRE TIMELINE AND REALITY – IS LESS ABOUT *WHAT* YOU CREATE AND MORE ABOUT THE MOVES YOU MAKE, RITUALS YOU CREATE, AND WHAT YOU EXPERIENCE, LEARN AND ALIGN WITH WHILE YOU CREATE IT. THE INNER, OFTEN UNSEEN LIFTS AND SHIFTS ARE WHAT BECOME THE SUPPORTIVE SCAFFOLDING THAT CAN HOLD THE OUTER REALITY IN PLACE. HERE'S WHAT HAPPENS WHEN YOU RECALIBRATE . . .

Narrative Shift

Your internal monologue, the storyteller that runs like an old vinyl record in your mind as truth, is (in my case at least) an unreliable narrator, yet we let it host the show. If your internal story says, "I never follow through", or "I'm too much/not enough", it's inevitable that your life will echo that belief. Rude, I know.

Self-creation begins by rewriting your origin myth. You choose a new role, a new voice, a new lens. One where you are the heroine/leading lady/queen (you decide), but you are absolutely not and never will be the footnote.

Ask yourself: What's the story I'm done living inside of? And what's the one I'm ready to create and narrate for myself? Write them both down, burn the first one and read the second over and over again, every single day.

Neurological Shift

In spiritual and somatic spaces the brain can often get a bad rap, but it's a very loyal life assistant: it repeats what's familiar, over and over.

So, what if you were to start visualizing, speaking and acting from your future self-creation? What if you gave your inner narrator a new script, one that was more in alignment with the reality you're respelling – and let the narrator know that this is very important and deserves all of your attention? You'd be teaching your brain a new reality to become loyal to and believe in.

Self-creation means rehearsing that new self until it becomes a reflex.

Ask yourself: What new truth am I willing to practise into permanence?

Emotional Shift

Your most rehearsed emotions become your creative palette. If you live in scarcity, abundance can feel . . . suspicious. If you're used to rejection, attention can feel dangerous. So if we're going to tell ourselves a different story (which we are), what emotions and scenarios would the version of our self-creation need as proof that we were experiencing them?

For me, I had to micro-dose "joy", because I absolutely did not trust it. (A lot of people in my life have died and the story I told myself was that if

I became *too* happy and experienced too much joy, someone else would die; I know, dramatic, but at the time it felt real.) So I had to recognize consciously what joy felt like and practise letting it be OK to be present in my body.

Self-creation means gently, in your own time and on your own terms, expanding your emotional range until joy, trust and self-belief feel like emotions that you can trust and experience regularly in your body.

Ask yourself: What emotion am I ready to normalize and experience more regularly as my "truth"?

Somatic Shift

Your body remembers what your mind conveniently forgets. If you try to leap between or collapse different potential timelines – to create and respell realities – while your nervous system still associates any form of expansion with danger, you'll sabotage yourself without even realizing it. It's why (and you'll read all about this as you move through the book) we start small to support a bigger nourishing and supportive process. We become devotional through rhythm and rituals, and slowly, rhythmically, we create something different, for ourselves and for each other.

Self-creation requires anchoring new identities in your body, not just in your mind.

Ask yourself: What would it feel like to be safe and successful?

Perceptual Shift

Your brain's reticular activating system (RAS) scans for what it is you most expect. Respell your reality and your mind will start to notice new opportunities and possibilities that you would've missed yesterday.

Self-creation rewires your radar. Your new self begins curating new evidence. **Ask yourself:** What am I finally available to see and experience?

Why Recalibration Is Key

Without recalibration, the act (and art) of self-creation essentially becomes a short-term dopamine high, the kind you get because you're in an "oh, I'm starting again" (and again) feedback loop. So life might momentarily look different, but it doesn't feel different, and the world – your reality – doesn't respond differently either. You may think you're declaring "this is who I am now!" really loudly, yet your body doesn't believe you, at least not right away.

When you're creating a new identity – and a new reality – the old ones will fight to survive. Sometimes this will look and feel really obvious; other times, it'll show up in insidious and sneaky ways, like self-doubt, resistance, emotional turbulence and external pushback. Those old stories know that your body simply cannot and will not hold a new level of visibility, love, success and/or power if it hasn't been shown that it's safe to do so. (FYI: This is why women often "manifest" what they want – most of us find that part really easy – only to reject it, self-sabotage or shrink once it arrives.)

The act of recalibration supports you in not collapsing back into old versions of yourself and helps you to steer clear of outdated realities. It's where the new is normalized and the bigness is regulated, so that you feel safe in the expansion – because it's in the expansion that your nervous system, emotional body and energetic field learn how to hold the frequency of the self that you're creating and the reality that you're respelling. Recalibration is your very own integration lab, where the self-creation process stabilizes and transformation gets encoded.

Some of us may find self-creation even trickier, because we're not just rewriting a story; we're having to unfreeze old ones. Unprocessed trauma, ancestral memory and/or identity scripts that we didn't choose, get stored in the body's fascia, the nervous system. If you experience a menstrual cycle, it can also get held, oftentimes really bloody uncomfortably (pun totally intended), in the emotional and physical experience of our period, too. When our system feels unsafe, the act and art of self-creation feel like a threat, and this is why no number of positive affirmations can, or ever will, override a body that's stuck in survival mode.

This is why we work *with* the body, because when we live and ritualize our rhythms and we create in sync with the Moon and menstrual phases, we become aware of and anchored in our own knowing, magic and wisdom. The deeper codes – the ones that are buried in fascia, scar tissue and skin – start to unfold and reveal, and it's here that our self-creation rewrites the rules.

Your nervous system learns that expansion is safe and you stop self-sabotaging at the first sign of success. (Hello, you finally start to keep the money that you manifest. Hurrah for that!) Pleasure and joy become your compass, and not a reward. Work, love and art all shift from patriarchal performance to true and real heart-led expression, burnout loses its grip and the lag between "dream life" and "daily life" collapses, so that the version of you that has the art show/podcast/farmhouse/French lover (add your own dream situ here) – the version of yourself that already exists in potential – rendezvous with you in reality much sooner.

Every choice, decision and shift you make places you in a different version of your reality.

THE POWER OF YOUR RHYTHMIC INTELLIGENCE

OUR RHYTHMIC INTELLIGENCE IS OUR INNATE, BODY-LED WISDOM THAT UNDERSTANDS AND EXPERIENCES TIME AS A CYCLE.

I've been teaching and sharing about the power of our cyclical nature – our menstrual magic, creative cycles and wild feminine rhythms – for over 20 years for a reason: because the logic of the straight line – produce, perform, progress, repeat – has been held as the societal/capitalist norm and has intentionally mislabelled a woman's cyclical and rhythmic intelligence as weakness, inconsistency and instability. We've been taught to override our tidal nature, mistrust our bodies, silence our intuition and imagination and prize the predictable over the powerful; basically, to go against everything that is supportive and nourishing and creative. But this intelligence – this deep, ancient way of knowing, relating and feeling – isn't transactional; it honours rhythms and rituals rooted in lunar, harvest and regenerative cycles and is the vital component necessary to respell your reality.

When we reclaim our cyclical nature, we disrupt the societal spell that commands that everything must be urgent, and we begin to live from our own centre. We stop contorting ourselves into the same societal cookie-cutter shapes and forms, and create our life around our own cycles, rhythms and creative pulses. We recognize that we're not consistent, but we're not inconsistent either. We just don't work to the 24-hour clock and Roman calendar (systems set up to control us); we're rhythmic, and so we trust the way that our energy and hormonal levels rise and fall, how our clarity and capacity to "see" deepens in the dark, and how our desire waxes and wanes like the Moon. We understand that creation doesn't always look like "doing" and being "productive"; sometimes it looks like waiting. Resting. Bleeding. Dreaming. Preparing the ground.

This remembering is an act of rebellion.

I do not need to be linear to be valuable.
I do not need to be consistent to be wise.

This is you, re-rooting into a kind of body-knowing that capitalism can't monetize, and patriarchy can't control and contain. (Although, believe me, they've definitely tried and will continue to do so!) It's a form of body-knowing that means you can name, stand for and live by your core values and beliefs. *Your* personal truth. A body-knowing that means that your self-respect and self-worth are so solid, so strong, that the moves, choices and decisions you make originate from *that* place.

To honour your rhythmic intelligence is to unhook from the systems and structures that thrive on our disconnection, and to root ourselves instead in the soil of our own magic, creative power and sovereignty. This is what protects us from being influenced and/or manipulated by, well, anything and anyone.

Because when a woman remembers, comes into relationship with and ritualizes her own rhythms, she remembers her power. Not the power to "keep up" and "keep doing", but the power to choose when, how, and whether to show up at all.

And that?

That changes everything.

WHEN WE SYNC WITH RHYTHMS AND NOT RULES

- **We stop** asking "Am I doing it right?"
  And start asking "Does this feel real and true in my body and my bones?"
- **We stop** measuring our worth in terms of output and checklists.
  And start recognizing the value that's held in how deeply we listen, rest, speak and are able to begin again.
- **We stop** trying to keep up with a system that was never built or created in our favour.
  And start remembering that our body is a sacred container for creative power and magic.
- **We stop** waiting for the perfect time, the perfect idea, the perfect energy.
  And start creating with the phases of the Moon, our menstrual cycle (if we experience one), the seasons and the cosmos.
- **We stop** panicking when our appearance changes.
  And start to understand that we're meant to age, mature and evolve.
- **We stop** abandoning ourselves on those days that we feel low, lost or tender.
  And start to cut ourselves some much-needed and well-deserved slack.

RHYTHMIC CREATIONS, RHYTHMIC REALITIES

THE MORE I LEARNED ABOUT MY OWN CYCLICAL NATURE AND THE RHYTHMIC INTELLIGENCE OF ALL THINGS, THE MORE APPARENT IT BECAME THAT THIS WAS ABOUT AN "ANTI-PRODUCTIVITY" APPROACH TO MY OWN CREATIVITY AND LIFE EXPERIENCE.

For the longest time, I was the self-proclaimed queen of perfectionism and procrastination, which, FYI, isn't an entirely great combination when it comes to writing books, making art and, well, having fun in life. Perfectionism and procrastination are symptoms of a woman trying to "create" in the patriarchal performance of productivity that we spoke about earlier, and which showed up for me in physical pain and mental contortion.

Over the years, I began to map and track my creativity and lived experience with my menstrual cycle, the cycle of the Moon, the seasons, planetary cycles (nothing was off limits, I'm a geek like that) and, of course, patterns emerged. I could get stuff done in the first half of my menstrual cycle, but after ovulation, it became much harder. When I chose to rest at menstruation and not push to be productive, I remembered how to dream and vision. (I describe how to map and track the menstrual cycle extensively in my books *Code Red* and *The Red Journal*.)

I shared this, along with other interesting patterns that I'd recognized, with the women I worked with, because many of them were trapped in shame-and-blame loops about starting something but not being able to finish it, and were also witnessing how this pattern showed up in different areas of their life. We all mapped and tracked our experiences in real time. It showed how certain moods, energy levels, desires, tendencies and emotions would show up in similar phases for each of us throughout each menstrual month.

I also worked with post-menopausal women as well as women who didn't experience a menstrual cycle, and we used the Moon and her phases (which can be mapped onto the phases of a menstrual cycle, along with the seasons) and the same thing happened. As we tracked the Moon's ebb and flow, similar fascinating patterns were emerging in the same phases of the Moon.

Over the years, all my books, work and art have been an invitation to return to our cyclical wisdom and rhythmic feminine intelligence, but what I haven't done (and that's mainly because I don't write anything as theory, but from the felt and lived experience) was share how I use this as a map to create. To access and activate my feminine frequency and respell my reality.

Moon-Based Quantum Fieldwork

What I refer to as the "feminine frequency" is a way of being and creating that honours rhythm, receptivity, intuition and emotion. It's cyclical, magnetic and embodied and aligned with the pulse of the Moon, your body, the Earth and your desires. It's feeling over force, ritual over routine and resonance over results, and while I'm by no means an expert on all things quantum (although *Quantum Leap* was one of my favourite TV programmes as a kid!), what I do know, because I've experienced it as true and real, is that the quantum is an energetic field of infinite potential. It's the space where all possible versions of reality already exist, waiting to be observed, felt, embodied and experienced, and it responds to:

- your vibration (how you feel)
- your self-concept (who you believe you are)
- your attention (what you observe, value and repeat)

By attuning to your feminine frequency, you fine-tune, align with and refine these variables; you anchor into your creative power (instead of survival loops and patterns); you access memories, dreams and desired futures from across lifetimes and timelines – all at the same time. And through rhythm, ritual and respelling, you become a vibrational match with a new version of your reality (one that's always existed) and the quantum field reorganizes itself accordingly.

At the quantum level, everything is energy and possibility – waves of pure potential are waiting to be collapsed into form. Science tells us that the very act of observation creates matter. Your attention is *not* passive; it's creative. What you focus on becomes real.

But what most of us were taught to believe is the opposite:

- Wait for the love to feel chosen
- Wait for the money to feel worthy
- Wait for permission, validation, clarity

That's the Newtonian model – the old-school, classic view of reality based on Isaac Newton's laws of physics – where the universe is seen as a predictable, mechanical system of cause and effect, hustle and grind, masculine logic ruling time and space. It works . . . but only up to a point. It's also what keeps women in a holding pattern.

Enter Moon-based quantum fieldwork: *this* is how we rhythmically (and rebelliously) respell reality. By working with the eight phases of the Moon as a living energetic template, you align your field with your own cyclical power. You collapse timelines by tuning your attention, energy and identity to the frequency of your deepest desires – phase by phase.

Moon-based quantum fieldwork gives us a living map to respell reality on our terms, in our own time, in harmony with something older, wilder, and far more intelligent than the algorithm or the to-do list.

For me, it's become the most playful and supportive container that's in alignment with the cycles of my body, the Moon, the seasons – and it's meant that through ritual and repetition, I now bring my art (and life) into form without force in ways that are sustainable, nourishing and fun. It's meant I've stopped fighting my natural energy and flow and started moving with it. I no longer see rest as "failure", because I know it fuels my capacity to imagine, dream and vision more of what's possible. I've stopped forcing my creativity to be switched on all the time, because I now trust with all my big, beat-y heart that each Moon phase serves my creativity – and it's here that something incredible happens: the act (and art) of creation gets easier. It becomes more pleasurable. More joyful.

So if you've felt the pull to create, to make, to express, to shape something beautiful – whether that's art, projects, or entire life shifts – but you struggle to fit into the rigid structures of traditional creativity guides (because let's be real: who needs another 12-week programme that you never actually finish? Come on, I *know* it's not just me!), then this approach is for you, too.

The Moon As Our Maven

Creativity, like us, doesn't move in a straight line. It's not a factory process (no matter what the tech bros would have us believe), we're not productivity "hacking" (don't get me started on *that* term), and it's definitely *not* a self-improvement plan. We don't need to "improve" anything; we simply need to become more alive and do all the things that conjure up that life force. No, this is a way of creating that honours, aligns with and reveres how magic and creative power and life force show up in our lives, so that we can respell reality.

THE MOON'S CYCLE OF CREATIVITY

Creativity moves through cycles, each one bringing its own energy, focus and purpose so that you can respell your reality, one phase at a time.

- **New Moon:** Dream. Imagine. Ideate. Vision. Set intentions. Dream bigger than you've dared before. Begin with boldness.
- **Waxing Crescent Moon:** Get curious. Play. Be fearless. Let curiosity lead you. Experiment wildly. Take playful steps toward your desires, even if they feel small.

- **Waxing Quarter Moon:** Dare and declare. Disciplined devotion. Declare your creative commitments out loud. Show up with fierce devotion to your craft and your vision.
- **Waxing Gibbous Moon:** Be your own muse. Take yourself (and your creativity) seriously. Refine your creations. Honour your process. See yourself as the powerful creatrix that you are.
- **Full Moon:** Innovate. Be seen. Express yourself. Shine unapologetically. Share your magic with the world. Celebrate your creative power in its fullness.
- **Waning Gibbous Moon:** Define. Refine. Align. (And discern.) Sharpen your vision. Align your energy. Release what no longer fits. Honour your clarity.
- **Waning Quarter Moon:** Revelations and revolutions. Embrace your inner rebel. Let truths rise and spark personal revolutions. Make powerful, aligned choices.
- **Waning Crescent Moon:** Reflect. Respect and celebrate. Pause. Honour your growth. Celebrate. Trust the cycle.

Charting Your Experience

When we think of the Moon, most people think of four phases: New, Waxing, Full and Waning. What's been exciting for me is that I've been diving deeper into this with the women I work with, and over the years we've explored how the eight phases of the Moon hold even more keys and codes to our creativity, self-creation and our ability to leverage the powers held in each phase to curate, conjure and respell our own realities.

Here's a simple step-by-step suggestion for how to chart and track a Moon cycle:

- Buy a journal or an exercise book or open a folder on your computer or phone and call it "Respell Your Reality".
- Get a Moon calendar so you can follow the Moon phases in real time. I prefer a paper version, but you can download the iLuna astrological app (and that's not an ad, although they absolutely should pay me – I pimp them in every book!) for smartphones that sends you notifications when the Moon moves from phase to phase and astrological sign to astrological sign in your time zone.
- Start each day by marking the following in your journal/notes:
  - date
  - Moon phase
  - astrological sign that Moon is in
- Chart your emotions – how you're feeling physically, mentally and spiritually.

- Chart your creativity; for example, this might be your word count on your work in progress. (You can make this a super-detailed exploration or a simple legend of symbols that are unique to you and your process.)

As you get to know each Moon phase, you may realize that you totally love the newness and space that's created at the New Moon, or the ability to get shit done in the first Quarter Moon. That's why your job now is to pay attention to all these discoveries, to chart them and to journal them as they unfold and reveal themselves to you, because they hold important clues about areas that may need more love or attending to on the ever-evolving creative process of being *you*!

What I share here in *Respell Your Reality* is a map for one complete Moon cycle. Eight phases. Eight creative movements. From dreaming to daring, to declaring, to celebrating, to resting and reflecting, it's a full creative arc, a complete spell.

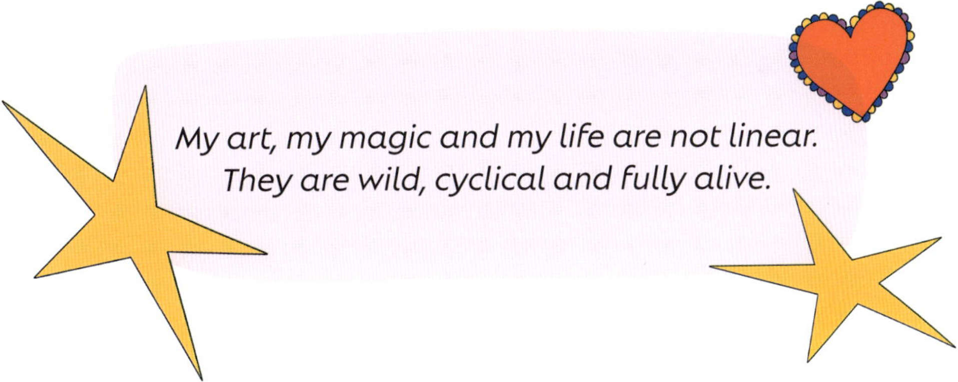

PART TWO

THE CREATIVE PHASES OF THE MOON

NEW MOON

DREAM. IMAGINE. IDEATE. VISION.

BE STILL.
CLOSE YOUR EYES.
THERE'S NO RUSH.
THERE'S NOWHERE TO BE.
EXCEPT HERE.
NOW.
KNOWING THAT IN EVERY MOMENT YOU ARE NEW,
YOUR REALITY IS NEW.
DREAM. WITH INTENT.
LET THAT INTENTION BECOME A DECLARATION OF FACT.
A STATEMENT SO TRUE AND STRONG THAT IT BECOMES A PORTAL
THROUGH WHICH MIRACLES AND MAGIC POUR IN.
RECEIVE.
ALLOW.
LET IT IN . . .

At the New Moon, we take the time to get still, we create space and we create comfort. (We eat cake, or a banana. We drink tea or green juice. Or gin. Your call.) We get out of our own way and we dare to dream. Big, bold, beauty-full dreams. We allow those dreams to take shape, and we let ourselves feel these dreams in our body and being, and declare – to ourselves and to the universe – *"I am a creatrix and I create What Comes Next."*

NEW MOON

- Your creative pulse begins to rise.
- Dream BIG dreams.
- Drink tea.
- Make space.
- Drink more tea.
- Eat chocolate.
- Allow for visions and downloads to take shape and form in the space of possibility.
- Set audacious and bold intentions and declare them so.

Sounds: Ambient, dreamy soundscapes. Think: Agnes Obel, Ólafur Arnalds, Sol Rising.

Essential oils and herbs: Clary sage (for visionary dreaming), lavender (for calm space-making).

Extra-sensory anchor: Soft textures like a cosy blanket or scarf, darkness, candlelight.

New Moon Energy and How It Affects You

The New Moon is the space where all possibility lives. You can't see it in the night sky – there's no light, no visibility, and that is the magic of it, because the New Moon is all about what's unseen: it's the cosmic womb of creation where your dreams, intentions and desires are imagined and conjured.

The New Moon phase asks:

WHAT DO YOU WANT TO CREATE?

It invites you to pause, be still and to dream wildly, audaciously and unapologetically. You have no interest in logic, strategy or plans in this phase, and are far more interested in ideation, imagining and dreaming.

It's in the New Moon phase that you are becoming the creatrix and spell-caster of your experience and reality, because it's here that you conceive and claim your desires; it's here when you let the pull of your big, beat-y heart point you in a direction that you might not have even yet considered.

Now please, for the love of Joan Jett, write those desires down. You can do this on the notes app on your phone if you wish, although there's something very alchemical that happens when you put pen to paper: a spell is cast and the cosmos *will* start to conspire.

This is a gorgeous time to be in the energetics of the void, the no-thing (where *anything* is possible), and get curious.

Ask yourself:

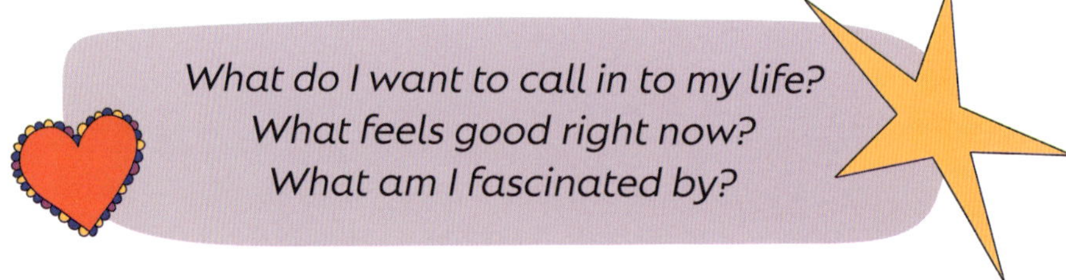

Let's be clear, this is absolutely NOT about writing a social media-worthy "goals" wish list and then crossing your fingers and hoping for the best. The New Moon phase is an opportunity to get real about what you truly desire and then to let yourself get really fascinated by it.

When we get fascinated by something, we're much more inclined to base future moves on our instinctual nature. We care less about what we think we "should" care about according to what we're told and sold, and instead we trust our hearts, our wombs (if we have them) and our unique-to-us frequency to be our guide. This can be risky in a world where we're taught to be compliant, but we're respelling reality and that means we're liberating ourselves from those stories and leaning into what freedom means to us, in the knowledge that each of us will have a totally different experience of it – and hurrah for that!

The New Moon phase is *not* the time for action-taking, move-making or "hustling" (although, personally, I'd suggest *no* time is good for hustling, but the New Moon is *definitely* not it.) It is, however, a time to rest, slow all the way down and go inward. We're rarely encouraged to rest, yet when we do, we're able to listen to our body and to get curious; because the creative energetics of the New Moon phase are raw. They're messy, without shape or form (and that's a good thing!). This is fertile ground where ideas are conceived and where our magic meets infinite potential.

There's no right or wrong here; it's just you and the vastness of all possibility. This is where the art of respelling reality and of rebellious and radical self-creation – the alchemy and the transformation – truly begins.

New Moon: A Riff

For years, I struggled with the same creative cycle: I'd have a big burst of creative energy, which would shortly be followed by burnout and a whole heap of half-finished projects that I would become far too overwhelmed to complete and I'd feel suffocated by the weight of my own doubt.

Working with the cyclical and rhythmic intelligence of the Moon means that I now use the New Moon phase to give myself something I hadn't allowed myself in years: permission to pause. Instead of chasing inspiration like it was some elusive, uncatchable "thing", I learned to wait, to sit still long enough to hear and feel my dreams and wishes make themselves known to me through my body, and then to ask questions – big, wild, messy questions – and be really OK with not having it all figured out right away.

So, at each New Moon, I now turn off every distracting device (of which I have a *lot*) and I sit with a blank page in my journal. I'm a big fan of keeping a diary and journaling because, yes, I'm a writer who loves to keep it old-school and write in inky pen on paper, but it's also where I can hear my own voice without interruption. I get to be contradictory. I get to change my mind. I get to be messy, mystical *and* mundane; and at the New Moon, without a plan or any fancy techniques, I simply let my pen move.

Words pour out, fragmented dreams, unspoken desires, ideas, flashes of images I can't quite make sense of yet. (And I've had to get really OK with not always having the words to articulate the whole "thing" right away.) Then, slowly, the threads *do* start to weave together. A new writing project, a series of art pieces. A short story idea. A vision for the creative life I want appears (and it's rarely, if ever, the one I thought I "should" have).

The New Moon phase is an opportunity to let myself dream without limitations.

To ideate without the pressure of making it perfect, without it having to be a complete and whole "thing" or having it all figured out. Now, I don't just stop at dreaming. I use the New Moon phase as a foundational space and place to plant the intentions and fragments of ideas and wishes and dreams and visions that I scribble in my journal like seeds, and I then use the energetics of each Moon phase that comes next to support those creative seeds in taking shape and form.

The New Moon has taught me, and continues to teach me every cycle, how important it is to trust the process and to trust myself. To try not to have it all figured out – no matter how much the control freak in me would love that – but to let there be space to rest, to dream and ideate. To let my imagination run wild, unburdened by the perceived need to "produce" and/or "perform".

Let the New Moon phase give you the courage to dream and imagine from a place of raw, unapologetic magic. *Your* raw, unapologetic magic.

Reclaim Your Imagination and Capacity to Dream

We've been taught to edit our dreams before they even fully form. We trade the wild expanse of our inner worlds for something that's perceived as much more "realistic", which, FYI, usually translates to something much smaller and much safer.

Why do you think there's been such a huge rise in women reading fantasy novels? Until recently, they weren't my thing, but lots of women who I really loved, admired and respected were raving about their favourite fantasy series – of which there are many! – so I became fascinated as to why. It couldn't just be about escapism and/or yearning for a hot fae king, could it? (Although, yes please, we're totally here for that!)

My conclusion has been that it's because when you're told often enough, as we have been and still are, that our magic and power are "made-up", fantasy becomes sacred ground.

In romantasy in particular, the central character is often a woman who realizes she's more than she was told she was. That she's not broken or small; she's powerful and magical; and it's in these stories and plot lines that we recognize new possibility for ourselves. Fantasy fiction lets us shape-shift, time-travel, enchant and be incredibly rebellious. (All my favourite things!)

I think there's also something really subversive in how these stories centre feeling, intuition, magic and deep inner knowing – the very traits that the over-culture has tried to downplay or pathologize in women. Fantasy restores and elevates them, making them essential to saving kingdoms, creating new ones and breaking curses. So I think we dig fantasy fiction because we're hungry for worlds that don't punish us for feeling, wanting and imagining. Which is why it's absolutely no surprise that fantasy, dreaming big and imagination, especially when associated with women, are often dismissed as indulgent, naïve or, worse still, delusional.

That word – delusional – has been weaponized against us for centuries. It's been used to discredit mystics, creatives, visionaries and anyone whose sense of what could be has threatened the status quo. In fact, it's the quickest way to make a woman doubt herself, doubt her power and doubt her own magic.

The cost of that conditioning?

We forget that our imagination is a tool of authorship, of reality construction, of self-creation. If we can't imagine new futures, new selves, new ways of being, then we can't build them. And *that* is the real danger of this cultural erosion of imagination: it severs us from our own creative power. If you can't see yourself somewhere other than where you are now, how can you ever move toward anywhere else?

Imagination lets us hold the world as it is in one hand, and begin sketching, dreaming into and envisioning the one that we long for and desire with the other hand. And when we reclaim it, we're not escaping or bypassing the current reality and our current experience; we're respelling and enchanting it as authors, creatrixes, spell-crafters and magic-makers with each and every dream, vision and creative longing we imagine.

The truth is, we're dreaming in a world that fears the fire of women who remember they can create; so please, for the love of all the women who have gone before (and who remind us that the conditions for creating are always less than optimal – thank you, Doris Lessing, for that observation),

BE AS DELUSIONAL AS MOTHER-LOVING POSSIBLE.

The Power and Benefits of the New Moon

The New Moon is the ultimate cosmic clean slate, inviting you to dream wildly and to envision what it is that you are being called to conjure and create. At the New Moon, while the sky is still dark, you can access your deepest intuition: *your wisdom*. Not information – that's what you'll find when you enter a subject into an online search engine. No, wisdom is what you *know*. It's the intel and insight stored in your body and being from lifetimes and timelines that, when you get still – when you trust yourself and the process, your magic and your power – will make itself known as big, bold dreams that are in alignment with your heart and with your truth.

The good news is that you don't have to have it all figured out; it's simply about opening yourself up to possibility. For creatrixes – us – especially, this is a chance to connect deeply with the cyclical, fertile energy of creation that is available to us *all*.

The New Moon phase offers a sacred container for dreaming and visioning *without limitation*.

NEW MOON

NIKI DE SAINT PHALLE (1930–2002)

"WHAT IS NOW KNOWN WAS ONCE ONLY IMAGINED."
NIKI DE SAINT PHALLE

Niki de Saint Phalle: artist, activist and a one-woman revolution. Her life was one big, technicolour middle finger to conformity and to everything that the over-culture tells us is "proper" or "possible". (High fives to that!) She was wild, she was brave and she was unapologetically messy, and that is precisely why she's our New Moon Maven.

Born in 1930, to a family that valued appearances over authenticity, Niki knew early on that she didn't fit their carefully curated life. Her dreams were too big, her ideas too bold, and her vision too vast. When life handed her pain – childhood trauma, mental health struggles, a world that couldn't make space for her – she alchemized the shit out of it. She turned it into art that was so wild, so alive, so unapologetically hers, that it rewrote the story of what art was or is supposed to be.

Niki created art *and* . . . she created entire worlds. Her bold Nanas – the voluptuous, larger-than-life sculptures of women bursting with colour and energy – are pure manifestations of her belief in the feminine as a source of power, joy and magic. Niki dreamed of a world where women could and would take up space; where their stories and bodies were celebrated instead of censored. And instead of waiting for someone else to create that world, she made it herself. Her Nanas were her manifesto: playful, bold and cheeky. They remind us that creativity doesn't have to be serious or polished to be revolutionary, it just has to be real.

What makes Niki the ultimate New Moon Maven is her commitment to the dream. She didn't just sketch ideas in a notebook and tell herself "one day" – she went all the way in. Niki dreamed and imagined the *Tarot Garden*, a sprawling sculpture park in Tuscany, Italy inspired by the cards of the tarot deck. It took her over 20 years to bring it to life, and while she faced challenges – financial struggles, physical injuries, criticism from those who could not see her vision – none of it stopped her from making it happen.

Because when you commit to the dream – *your* dream – you show up for it no matter what and you do *not* wait for someone else to give you permission.

Niki *never* asked for permission. She also never waited for someone to validate her ideas *and* she didn't wait until she was "ready" either.

She simply started. She picked up a gun, shot at paint-filled bags attached to a canvas, and called it art. She transformed her pain into beauty, her rage into colour, her ideas into monuments that will stand long after we're gone.

Niki reminds us that creation is messy, chaotic and gloriously imperfect, and *that* is where its magic lies.

So, as you enter the New Moon phase, let your heart riff on the following questions:

- What's the dream I've been afraid to say out loud?
- What's the wild, technicolour idea that's been living in my heart, waiting for me to pick up a metaphorical paint-filled gun and go for it?

Let Niki be your inspiration to dream it, to ideate it, to create it. Big. Bold. Messy. Your personal Nana, bursting with magic and possibility, because the world you long for isn't just possible – it's waiting for YOU to make it real.

The Hot Spots and Shadows of the New Moon

While the New Moon definitely brings promise and potentiality, there's no denying that the expectation of what's to come can feel overwhelming. The darkness of the Moon mirrors our inner shadows, and that can stir up feelings of uncertainty or doubt. You may find yourself questioning your worth, your desires, or your actual ability to create, manifest and make things happen. These doubts ultimately want to keep you safe, yet they're blocking your dreams, so witness them as an opportunity to confront your fears and insecurities.

Another hot spot? The New Moon's energy is quiet and still, which can potentially feel "unproductive" or frustrating in a world that loves to worship the hustle. The temptation to rush into action or to figure it all out can prevent you from fully sinking into this phase's magic.

My advice? Don't let it.

Mistress Your Magic

You don't mistress your magic by thinking about it. You mistress it by *building a relationship* with it, like you would with a lover, a creative practice or your own body. Here are some practices and rituals to support you in becoming an energetic frequency match with the New Moon phase.

New Moon Creative Visioning Session

To connect with your intuitive creativity and open yourself to possibility.

You'll need

- A blank canvas or sheet of paper
- Paints, markers or any creative tools you love to use

1. Set up a sacred space for creating by lighting some incense, playing your favourite music, or simply sitting by candlelight.
2. Take a few minutes to close your eyes and envision what it is you desire to create in this cycle. Don't rush; let images, colours or feelings come to you naturally.
3. Open your eyes and start creating on your blank canvas or paper. This isn't about making "art"; this is about translating your vision into something tangible. Use colours, shapes or words that feel alive and meaningful to you.
4. Once you've finished, sit with your creation and ask yourself:
   - What does this say about my desires?
   - How can I nurture this energy in the coming days?
5. Display this piece somewhere you'll see it daily to remind you of the magic you're creating, manifesting and shaping into form.

The Dream Bowl Ritual

To clarify your intentions and plant seeds of creation.

You'll need

- A small bowl
- Water
- A few fresh petals from a flower of your choice (I always use roses because they are heart medicine to me and white roses especially are perfect for new beginnings; also, blue lotus petals are great for enhancing dreams – you could use a few blue lotus petals in this ritual and then use the rest to make a tea infusion that will amplify your dream experience)
- A candle (preferably white to represent a fresh start)
- A journal or piece of paper
- A pen

1. Begin in a quiet space. Light a candle (yes, you *are* a grown-up, but it never hurts to be reminded never to leave a candle unattended and to keep it away from flammable materials), and take a few deep breaths to ground yourself.
2. Place the bowl of water in front of you and scatter the petals on its surface, symbolizing your dreams.
3. Speak your intentions aloud as if they are already so. For example, you could say: "My creative work flows with ease and impact", letting your voice vibrate with power and belief.
4. Spend a few moments gazing at the water, imagining your desires coming to life. Visualize them as clearly as possible.
5. Write these intentions down and reflect on how you want them to feel. Remember, the New Moon is about feeling into possibility, not over-thinking.
6. Extinguish the candle safely to seal the ritual and leave the bowl overnight under the dark sky.
7. In the morning, pour the water into the earth – on a plant you love – as an offering, knowing that your intentions are ready to grow. If you don't have a garden, find a tree in your local park or pour it into an indoor plant pot.

The Body Blessing

To embody your creative power and align with your energetic frequency.

You'll need:

- Your favourite essential oil (diluted in a carrier oil) or body lotion
- A candle (white is great for energetic clarity)
- A quiet space
- A mirror

1. Stand in front of your mirror and light a candle. Look at yourself without judgement: this is your vessel of magic, creation and power.
2. Rub a few drops of the oil or lotion into your hands and as you touch each part of your body, speak blessings over it, such as:
   - Thank you, hands, for bringing my creations into the world.
   - Thank you, heart, for holding my dreams and desires.
   - Thank you, feet, for carrying me toward my vision.
3. Feel the energy move and shift as you honour and really love up your body as a sacred vessel of creation.
4. Close the ritual by placing your hands over your heart and saying:

   I am the creatrix of my reality.
   I trust my magic, my vision and my power.

5. Blow out the candle to seal the ritual.

NEW MOON: THE FIELD OF POSSIBILITY

Intention · Imagination · Identity Reset

The Science: At the subatomic level, where everything begins as vibration, you are mostly empty space – a field of probability and possibility waiting to take shape and form. Nothing is fixed until it is observed, so who do you *observe* yourself to be right now?

The Magic: This is your cyclical blank-page moment where you remember that you, your life and experience are your own self-creation. Your timeline is still a dream. What you dare to desire *will* send a ripple out through the field.

The Respell: Choose, imagine and *feel* the frequency of what wants to be created, and conjure the version of yourself who already exists and is waiting to be observed in the darkness of possibility. She's listening.

Remember that respelling your reality is a process. Be in it, show up and drop expectations – of yourself, of this process, of this entire experience.

This phase of the Moon demands space and stillness so that your dreams and ideas can take form. It's a place and space to set intentions, but you don't need to "think" them into being – that's a very hit-or-miss style of manifestation – no, what we're doing here is working with the New Moon phase to create space for possibility. We're allowing ourselves to slow all the way down and honour ourselves and our bodies as a vessel of magic, creation and power.

Many people hear "New Moon" and immediately think they have to do something – set goals, make moves, take action. We're conditioned to strive and push; that's familiar terrain. But the real invitation of the New Moon is to pause. To let the stillness do its work.

It's in that quiet, receptive space that we become magnetic – where we allow, attract and begin to respell reality from the inside out.

WAXING CRESCENT MOON

GET CURIOUS. PLAY. BE FEARLESS.

LET YOUR VISIONS, DREAMS AND INSIGHTS GUIDE
YOU INTO A SPACE OF FECUNDITY AND PLAY.
LET THEM BECOME SEEDS WITH ROOTS THAT WILL S L O W L Y
TAKE SHAPE AND FORM IN THE NOURISHED SOIL OF CURIOSITY,
PLAY, WONDER AND DELICIOUS NAIVETY.
SUPPORT AND PROTECT AND NURTURE THOSE IDEA
SEEDS AS THEY GROW STRONG ROOTS . . .

This is the phase to allow your dreams and visions and ideas to take form. How? By creating a fecund and nourishing landscape for ideas, dreams and visions to grow and expand.

But how do we do that? By sourcing ourselves. By making time and space to play. By honouring yourself and the ideation process. (I know it's a wanky advertising word, but it's *exactly* what this Moon phase is all about: the formation of ideas and concepts.)

WAXING CRESCENT MOON

- Play.
- Be curious.
- Make no judgement.
- Get messy.
- Contain exposure.
- Nurture yourself.
- Become fecund.
- Nurture your ideas.
- Prepare.
- Practise ideation (yes, it's a "thing").

Sounds: Playful, uplifting beats. Think: Florence and The Machine, Maggie Rogers, Lizzo.

Essential oils and herbs: Sweet orange (for joy and brightness), peppermint (to awaken curiosity).

Extra-sensory anchor: Movement – dance in your kitchen, shake it out, march on the spot; moving your body in a way that feels good will ignite your creative spark.

Waxing Crescent Moon Energy and How It Affects You

The Waxing Crescent Moon is where the spark of potential ignites. If the New Moon is the space of dreaming and planting seeds, then this phase is when you start to see those seeds start to grow roots. It's a tender time, delicate and full of raw possibility. This is the phase where curiosity meets courage, where you dare to believe in your dreams and begin to shape them into something real.

This phase is all about momentum. It's that first burst of energy after the stillness of the New Moon. To be clear, momentum does *not* mean you have to dive straight into making things happen. Nope, the Waxing Crescent Moon is an experimental time. It's full of twists and turns and what-ifs, maybes and fail-forwards. It's the phase where you get to throw paint at the canvas, scribble ideas in the margins, and let your imagination run wild without worrying about the end result. You're not here to create a masterpiece. Yet. (If ever.)

No; right now, you're here to play.

The Waxing Crescent Moon is a mischievous minx whispering, "Go on, try it. See what happens. I dare you." It invites you to be fearless in your exploration, to dare to follow the threads of inspiration wherever they lead.

What do you want to explore?
What feels exciting?
What would you do if you weren't worried about getting it right?

What this phase *isn't* about is big, bold leaps. It's about the tiny, intentional actions that build momentum over time. It's writing the first paragraph of a story, doodling in your sketchbook, or signing up for that course you've been wanting to try. Every small act of creation is sending out a super-clear signal across lifetimes and timelines – the quantum field – that you're serious about becoming an energetic match for your dreams.

Now, this phase *can* bring up resistance. You might hear that little voice in your head saying, "Who are you to do this? What if it doesn't work out?" And that's normal. The Waxing Crescent Moon is a phase that invites to you to dance with your doubts and choose curiosity over fear (which is *definitely* a daily practice, but one that you really get to explore and experiment with in this phase).

So, how do you work/play with this energy? Start by asking yourself:

What am I curious about right now?

Then follow that. It doesn't need to make sense. In fact, it probably won't. It doesn't need to be perfect; chances are it absolutely won't be. You just need to start. Take one step, then another. Play. Explore. Let yourself be surprised.

The Waxing Crescent Moon holds the energy of "what if?" and your work or play isn't going to have all the answers; it's about discovering them as you go along.

Waxing Crescent Moon: A Riff

Perfectionists and control freaks (I'm addressing myself here) may find this phase . . . um . . . tricky. I used to *really* struggle with it, because the big dreams that I'd conjure during the New Moon felt safe in the dark, hidden where no one could see, witness or, more importantly, judge them. Yet, when the first light of the Waxing Crescent Moon appeared in the night sky, so would the questions:

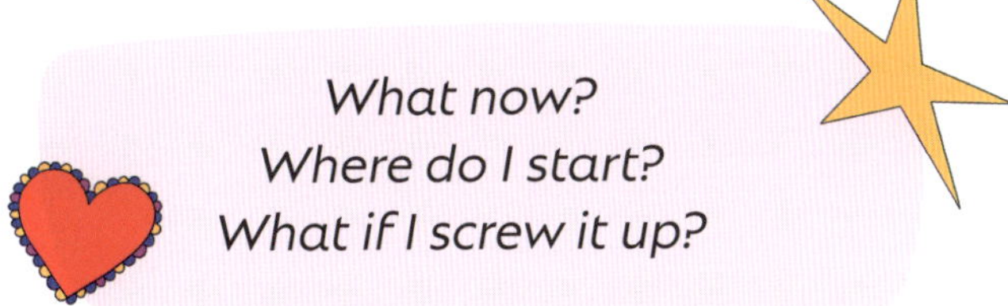

I have no problem with ideas. My notebooks, diaries and journals have always been full of sketches, riffs, book and project ideas – everything from movie scripts to jewellery designs, to the name of the perfect red in my yet-to-be-created make-up range – and for the longest time, that's where those ideas stayed: on paper, tucked away for "one day". However, what I can confirm is that there are published books and art and oracle decks in the world, created by me, because of the Waxing Crescent Moon phase.

This phase has *no* interest in "one day" or in waiting for some mythical perfect moment. It calls you to simply start. Yes, doubt will inevitably creep in: *What if it doesn't come out the way I want? What if no one likes it?* But this phase is not about perfection. I repeat: *this phase is not about perfection.* It's about curiosity, play and taking small steps.

This is how I got past the paralysis that came with overthinking and worrying about the final outcome. This is how I let the process of creation

be playful. (Because, FYI, it absolutely must be playful; otherwise, what's the point?) I tried different techniques I'd been curious about but hadn't dared to attempt before. Some worked. (I love watercolour painting; it's now my main meditation source.) Some didn't. (Turns out acrylics aren't my jam.) But each movement I made during this Moon phase brought me closer to the act and art of creating, versus staying "safe" in the dream phase.

As the Waxing Crescent Moon grows, so will your momentum. What I've found is that an idea – whether it's words on a page, colouring pens on paper – will evolve because it's inspired by my willingness to get messy and try. My perfectionism, the thing that has loved to keep me safe but mostly keeps me stuck, loosens its grip. When I realized that I didn't have to have the whole thing figured out before I took the first step and that I just had to start, ideas started to take actual shape and form.

We've been brilliantly and, in some cases, brutally led to adhere to the systems that worship output, metrics and certainty – this was definitely how it was for me – and when we think that way, curiosity becomes a liability and play looks like procrastination. But what I absolutely now know to be true is that nothing truly original, nourishing and/or beautiful comes from relentless control. I have zero interest in spreadsheets; I want seduction, surprises and, ideally, a lot of silliness.

How did I change it up? I reframed play as practice and set up low-stakes creatrix dates with myself. If you're writing, doodling, collaging or dancing in your kitchen, you're *not* wasting time – you're loosening the creative muscles and tuning in. Give yourself permission to create what I lovingly refer to as "small rituals of sanctioned delight", aka 20-minute windows to follow a weird idea, where nothing has to be good. Nothing has to be posted online. Nothing has to be done. Finger-paint, try a new tool, dance to a playlist you've made, or make something utterly pointless.

I created small rituals of sanctioned delight, because I equated stillness with slacking and experimentation with failure, so my body needed to be gently re-educated (with love). This 20-minute window, a few times a week, is what helped me to develop trust in myself as a creatrix. I learned that it was safe to be messy, safe to wonder, safe not to know.

Do you know what else I learned? That playfulness is productivity in disguise. The more curious you are, the more energy you have. The more relaxed you are, the more ideas arrive. Curiosity is the doorway to creative flow, and when you stop trying to "get it right", you let it get interesting – and that's how I redefined time.

Linear time, patriarchal time, "time is money" time? That's not my calendar. I work on Moon time. And on *that* timeline, anything that nourishes your soul is productive. Because it produces more YOU-ness.

Go wild, be unproductive and gloriously waste time.

Ideation

"Ideation" sounds like one of those marketing terms you'd hear in a beige brainstorming room with flickering fluro lights, bad coffee and a whiteboard. But stripped of its corporate suit, ideation is a useful and real part of the Waxing Crescent Moon phase. Simply put, ideation means the act of generating ideas. If we let it, it can be messy, magical and sometimes chaotic – and it's where sparks fly, creative fires get lit and you start to sense the shape of what could be.

Good news: when we ideate we don't need or require a "strategy deck" or Post-it notes (though you can use them if they light you up). For our purposes, ideation is much more rooted in embodiment and desire – like daydreaming in the bath, scribbling in the margins of your journal, noticing a phrase that makes your heart jump and dedicating an entire poem to it, or being struck by the scent of something that takes you back to a memory that's begging to become an entire story.

It's about getting curious and playful and what it is you sense and *feeeeel* in response to it all.

The Power and Benefits of the Waxing Crescent Moon

The Waxing Crescent Moon is where curiosity and play become powerful antidotes to fear. It's where instead of asking, "What if I fail?", I now ask, "What if I try?" That shift changed everything for me, because it means you're no longer imagining possibilities; you're actively shaping them.

The Waxing Crescent Moon is the first light after the dark New Moon. It's when your ideas shift from abstract to "Oh, this might actually be something." The important thing to remember is that the Waxing Crescent Moon phase isn't asking or demanding proof that this will "work"; it's simply asking you to show up, not because you know exactly what to do or where an idea may go, but because you understand that it *will* build momentum.

Momentum matters, because without it, dreams, visions and ideas can remain stuck in limbo. This Moon phase reminds us that motion doesn't have to be dramatic to be effective. Small acts, repeated, generate a rhythm. Writing a paragraph, making a playlist for your project, collecting visual references and setting up your space are all momentum in action. So consider this phase the time to nourish and tend to your dreams and ideas gently – without coercion, force or fear of failure. I now use the Waxing Crescent Moon phase as my personal permission slip to explore, experiment and play every Moon cycle. It's the phase where I say yes to my ideas without needing them to be perfect.

Each small move you make during this phase shifts you from the dreaming phase, fuels your creative fire and sends ripples out through time and space, into the quantum field. When it becomes clear that you're ready to bring your dreams into reality, the quantum rearranges itself accordingly to respell and support you. This phase holds enormous potential, but only if you're willing to show up, play and say yes to what's possible (which is *everything*)!

WAXING CRESCENT MOON MAVEN

BEATRICE WOOD

(1893–1998)

"I OWE IT ALL TO ART BOOKS, CHOCOLATE AND YOUNG MEN."
BEATRICE WOOD

Beatrice Wood devoured life. She was an artist, sculptor, writer and all-round bad-ass who lived to be 105 years old. When asked the secret to her longevity, she famously quipped, "art books, chocolate and young men". *This* is the energy we all need to tap into during the Waxing Crescent Moon.

Beatrice didn't play by the rules. (We love her for that!) She didn't follow a pre-approved path to success. She didn't care about perfection and she certainly didn't care what people thought of her. What she *did* care about was curiosity, play and following what felt good and letting her passions be her guiding force throughout her entire life. That's exactly why she's our Moon maven for this phase, because she shows us how to explore the world without fear of failure, judgement or limits.

Born in 1893, Beatrice was expected to marry well and to stay within the confines of polite society. Spoiler alert: she didn't. She ran away to Paris (my kinda woman!), got involved in the Dada art movement (which was all about breaking the rules of art and life) and threw herself into creating pottery, paintings and writings that were as eccentric and unique as she was.

Beatrice didn't wake up with a perfectly formed plan or blueprint for her creative work; no, she played. She got her hands dirty. She experimented. She made messes and magic in equal measure. She followed her curiosity, no matter how bizarre or unconventional it seemed. In her forties, she randomly decided to take a pottery class, and what started as a casual interest became a lifelong passion that went on to make her world famous.

Beatrice and her life and art are proof that you don't need to know exactly where you're going; you simply have to start exploring and experimenting. Pick up the paint brush. Open the notebook. Book a trip to a place that you've never been but feel called to. Follow the thread of an idea and see where it takes you. The Waxing Crescent Moon phase invites you to do just that: play, experiment, and let your creativity flow without needing it to be perfect.

Beatrice was fearless. She wasn't afraid to make bold choices. She wasn't afraid to make weird art or live outside society's expectations. She wasn't afraid to reinvent herself – again and again – and she shows us that curiosity trumps fear every time. When you're curious, you don't have time to be scared. You're too busy asking: *What if? What next? How far can I take this?*

The magic of Beatrice's legacy is her playful approach to life. She reminds us that we don't have to wait until we're "ready" to start creating. We just have to be brave enough to begin and to trust that the act of creation will reveal what's next. So, during the Waxing Crescent Moon phase, channel Beatrice.

Get messy. Try new things. Say yes to what excites you, even if you've absolutely no idea where it'll lead (*especially* if you have no idea where it will lead)! Follow the threads of your curiosity and let yourself be surprised by where those threads do lead you.

And for the love of *She*, remember Beatrice's words: "Art books, chocolate and young men." This doesn't have to be your own combination – although personally, I'm very much in favour of it! – but know and trust that life, like art, should be delicious, playful and fearlessly lived on *your* terms.

The Hotspots and Shadows of the Waxing Crescent Moon

While this phase is full of possibility, it's also where, as I've previously mentioned, doubt and resistance *can* start to creep in. You've set your intentions and declared them out loud, but now that things are moving, the voices of self-doubt might say: *What if it's not good enough? Who do you think you are to do this? What if I fail?*

The shadows of the Waxing Crescent are wrapped in fear of imperfection and procrastination disguised as "I'm just not ready yet". You might find yourself waiting for more clarity or confidence, thinking you need to figure it all out before taking action – but guess what? The clarity you're seeking comes through the doing, not before it.

Another potential shadow? Burnout before you even begin. You might want to do all the things all at once, rushing to see results, but the Waxing Crescent teaches us to pace ourselves and trust the process. Remember what we discovered during the New Moon phase? You don't need to have all the answers before you start creating. Recognize when you're stalling and/or procrastinating and take any small action to break the cycle. For example, I often set a timer for 20 minutes and tell myself to take the first step. Create for the joy of it, without pressure to finish or be perfect.

The final hotspot I need to highlight is sharing an idea before it's ready. It's tempting during this phase, because you're so excited and full of the idea and its possibility that you want to share it with others; but it's still in seed form and if you share it too soon, it might not have had enough time to take root. Sharing it with others and opening it up for critique and feedback at such an early stage can lead to the fire, excitement and passion being extinguished prematurely. You risk losing momentum because you've spent more time sharing and less time tending.

Mistress Your Magic

Here are some practices and rituals to support you in becoming an energetic frequency match with the Waxing Crescent Moon phase.

Create a Curiosity Map

To tap into curiosity and explore possibilities without fear of judgement or failure.

You'll need:

- A large sheet of paper or your journal
- Markers, pens and/or coloured pencils
- A big open heart and mind

1. Start by drawing a big circle in the middle of your paper and write: "What am I curious about?"
2. Around the circle, draw smaller circles and write whatever comes to mind – ideas, dreams, questions, wild and "out there" thoughts. Don't overthink this; for example: "learning to play guitar", "launching a creative project", "exploring new art styles", "travelling solo".
3. Once your map is filled with possibilities, choose one curiosity that feels the most exciting and ask: "What's one small way I can explore this curiosity today?"
4. Take a playful action toward that curiosity, without any pressure for it to be perfect.

The First Step Ritual

To break through resistance, self-doubt and procrastination by making micro-moves.

You'll need:

- A candle (preferably white or yellow to symbolize new beginnings)
- Your journal or a blank piece of paper
- A pen
- A small object (like a crystal, charm or coin) to serve as a talisman

1. Create a quiet space, light your candle and say out loud:

   This light symbolizes my first step. I trust the process, I trust myself and I make moves that are in the direction of forwarding life and in alignment with my desires.

2. Close your eyes for a few moments and sit with the declaration. Now, without overthinking, write down the smallest possible move you can make that would prove to yourself: "Look, I'm showing up!"

3. Hold the small talismanic object you've chosen and say:

   This talisman holds my commitment to making this move. I move forward with curiosity and courage.

4. Place the object in your workspace, on your bedside table, or turn it into a necklace (depending on what it is, obviously!) as a reminder of your self-commitment.

5. Blow out the candle to seal the ritual. Now, go make that move.

The Curiosity Cabinet Ritual

Think of this as creating a living altar to your wonder.

1. Find a small box, a large jar, a corner of your desk, a pin board, a journal spread or even a folder on your phone or laptop. This is now your curiosity cabinet – your personal portal to everything that fascinates you!
2. Each day during the Waxing Crescent Moon phase, offer it something interesting. A scrap of an overheard conversation. A receipt from somewhere unexpected. A quote that hit you straight in the heart. A song lyric that you have on repeat. A scribbled idea. Anything that tickles or tugs at your awareness.
3. Each time you add to a new object, ask: What if this means something? What might it want me to make, feel or remember? Don't force answers, just let the question open the door wider. You're not trying to do anything with this yet. The practice is in collecting, honouring and staying close to the edge of what excites you. This is pre-logic, pre-linear, pre-production magic.
4. When you feel stuck, go to your cabinet. Use it as an oracle. Close your eyes, reach in and pull something out. Let it take you on an adventure – is this the start of a poem? Is it evoking a memory that wants to be turned into a piece of music?
5. This ritual practice isn't about outcomes; it's about keeping the creative channel open while nourishing and intriguing it in the process.

WAXING CRESCENT MOON: TUNE IN

Desire · Belief · Magnetic Initiation

The Science: Quantum theory tells us that "the field" (the invisible, energetic vibrating fabric of the universe where all timelines and possibilities exist until you collapse one into form) responds to coherence. Your focus – what you look at, feel, expect and experience – creates a vibrational frequency.

The Magic: Here, your desires become magnetic. So forget logic and proof; you need *resonance*. Begin aligning your thoughts, emotions and attention with the version of reality that you desire.

The Respell: Amplify your unique-to-you frequency – *your* signal – by observing the outcomes that you desire. What desire feels totally illogical and also really exhilarating right now? What thought or emotion would match the version of you who is already living and experiencing that reality?

Let curiosity, not perfectionism, be your guide. The Waxing Crescent Moon phase is not about perfection or having all the answers – it's about showing up and letting your ideas take shape in real time.

Ask yourself:

What feels fun?
What lights me up?
What would I try if I wasn't afraid?

This is your playful phase. Your experimental, don't-take-it-too-seriously phase. Really, truly, you're *allowed* to be excited and fascinated. Often. It's not finite.

Your creative power is already within you and during the Waxing Crescent Moon phase you get to practise trusting it, taking one step at a time, playing and experimenting and acknowledging and celebrating every move you make, every step you take, no matter how small, because it counts.

Stir your creative cauldron by flirting with possibility, getting excited and enjoying and following the thrill that comes with not knowing yet but feeling the fizz of "Oh, this *feeels* like something good!"

WAXING QUARTER MOON

DISCIPLINED DEVOTION

FEEL THE TENSION BETWEEN THE DREAMS AND VISIONS YOU HAVE, YOUR DESIRE AND PASSION, YOUR LIT CREATIVE FIRE AND THE DISCIPLINED DEVOTION AND RITUALIZED REPETITION REQUIRED TO RESPELL REALITY. THIS IS THE MOMENT YOU SAY: *"YES, I CHOOSE THIS. YES, I CHOOSE ME."*

Let yourself command and compel and code your commitment direct from your heart, with your whole chest, so that your action is devotional and is in direct response to the ancient/future drumbeat of your feminine frequency.

Declare it.

Dare it.

Devote yourself to it.

This phase is the spring equinox of the Moon phases; it's when we see nature start to come to life after the winter and it's when our dreams seed, if they've been tended to and nourished, and they commit to shape and form. This is where we dive all the way in. We've played and we've experimented and now it's here, at the Waxing Quarter Moon phase, that we make a commitment to do what's necessary to bring the intentions that we made at the New Moon into being.

WAXING QUARTER MOON

- Create.
- Hurl yourself into life.
- Be. In. The. Process.
- Take risks.
- Be in action.
- Trust what it is you desire.
- Live passionately (as in really live, so you have something to write/talk/create about).

Sounds: Power anthems. Think: Beyoncé's "Run the World (Girls)", Sia's "Unstoppable", Alicia Keys' "Girl On Fire".

Essential oils and herbs: Rosemary (focus and determination), ginger (courage).

Extra-sensory anchor: Writing and creative tools that you love and that support your process; I *never* need an excuse to buy stationery, and if it can be both pretty *and* functional, that makes showing up to the page an even more pleasurable *and* devotional experience!

Waxing Quarter Moon Energy and How It Affects You

We're now at the mid-point between New Moon and Full Moon: the Waxing Quarter Moon. Take a look at it in the sky if you can: half will be in darkness, half will be in light. As the Moon waxes, so too will your ideas. This is a phase of tension, friction and choice. It's where energy builds and the dreamy and playful nature of the New and Crescent Moons either fizzles out or finds form.

Creatively, this is where momentum meets resistance, and while I admit that doesn't sound great, it's not a bad thing. In fact, it's necessary. This phase mimics the moment in any creative process when that initial rush of inspiration begins to rub up against doubt, distraction and real-world logistics. Maybe you've sketched out a new idea, started a project or made a commitment to yourself, and now it feels a bit wobbly? The Waxing Quarter Moon asks/invites/arse-kicks you to get real about what you want to bring into the world. It's where you start to question: *Is this worth it? Can I really do this?*

Yep, it's a time to make decisions and bold moves, and to commit. FYI, there's a good chance you still have no idea as to how it will end, yet you still have to make a choice – and that will take courage. This phase has got a bit of guts about it, reminding us that creative work often requires some resistance training, so that we can work with friction rather than running from it. For example, you might feel tension between your idea and your time. Between your desire and your fear. Between what you've done before and what you're being called to do now. The Waxing Quarter Moon is where we build. It's where we ground and stabilize our creative force with real-world scaffolding. It's where you get to give your idea a container. Give your dream a schedule. Choose a title. Pick a palette. Start the damn draft.

This is the phase that most of the women I work with favour, because it's known territory. Society favours the things this Moon phase represents – all things fresh, new and productive – which makes this phase feel more comfortable. It affords us the energy to "comply" and "function" in line with the structures in which we're familiar. The expanding light of the Waxing Quarter Moon can lift your energy as you shrug off the winter coat of the Dark and New Moons and step into the newness of this spring-like energy.

So in this lunar phase the energy is assertive, directional and a little defiant. You commit, you make choices, you "do". This is your "get-shit-done" phase.

Waxing Quarter Moon: A Riff

This is a juicy one because I love to dream; I *love* to ideate. The New Moon and Waxing Crescent are comfy spaces for me to spend my time, but it turns out, I *might* have commitment issues. I love the shiny possibility of new ideas; I collect them like a creative magpie: I sketch rough outlines of art I'm going to make, plot entire fiction series from start to finish, make mood boards and compile playlists for places I'm going to live in the world . . . but then, inevitably, comes the energetic nudge: *OK, what now? What are you going to commit to? Are you going to do it, or are you going to let it slip away?*

It's at this point we can feel both excitement and terror in equal measure. You love the idea. But sharing it with the world? Actually doing it? Committing to it? Well, that requires a whole new level of courage, right?

Now, I'm by no means a creative monogamist, I don't think I ever will be, and I would still very much prefer not to start anything until *all* the conditions are perfect and I know exactly where I'm going and I have proof that my idea will work, but spoiler alert: *that will never happen*. What I do know is that a considerable number more of my creative projects (in art and life generally) get started and completed (this one included!) because I use the Waxing

Quarter Moon phase to commit and show up and start before I'm ready. (FYI, I'm never really ready.)

My secret sauce? I've cultivated disciplined devotion, showing up for my magic again and again, even when it feels scary. Even when doubts creep in. Even when I don't know exactly where it's going. Now, I did say in my book *Self Source-ery* that it's devotion over discipline every single time, and while I stand by that, I've found that in order to *really* show up for myself and my magic, I need a collaboration between the two. (The joys of being me and you being you is that we can change our minds *any* time – hurrah!)

I love disciplined devotion because it's magic *and* it's mundane. I need the structured, intentional effort (discipline), and I also need heartfelt, passion-driven creativity, ritual and flow (devotion). It's the combination of the two, merging the sacred and the practical, that takes something like this book, for example, from a good concept to actual words on the page, to the physical copy you're now reading.

So what exactly is disciplined devotion? It's about making the conscious choice to back yourself, your magic and your creative process, even when that feels messy or uncertain. It's a loving back rub to yourself that says: *I'm here for this. I'm here for myself. I trust myself enough to keep going.* It's aligning with the waxing and waning, the expansion and contraction rhythms of our cyclical experience, and honouring the process by building creative rituals that support us. Whether it takes the shape of writing each morning, pulling a daily tarot card or spritzing a scent that you associate with the life you're creating, it's about the rituals that keep you grounded in your creative power and support your rhythm and ways of showing up.

Whether you're writing a book or moving to a new locale, you need a balance of fierce commitment to yourself and your project and compassionate flexibility for when life inevitably throws you curveballs. While some days you might take bold action, and on others you may need to rest, reflect and tend to your inner world, you're ultimately looking to shift from dreaming about what you want to create, to doing what's required to make it real.

So while the New Moon invites you to dream and the Waxing Crescent asks you to explore, the Waxing Quarter Moon is where you declare your commitment and take action. This is about trust and intuition and not about tried and tested formulas and paths to success.

This is *your* daily devotion. To you. When you choose to devote (with discipline) to your creative magic, you learn to trust that your creative power is worth showing up for. That *you* are worth showing up for.

Cultivating Courage

Perhaps you're being called to speak up and out. To sing *your* song. Even if it sounds different to the mainstream narrative. To tell a different story to the one that you've been told. To walk where there may not currently be a pathway – and now it's up to you to clear the brambles and take down the "do not enter" sign, which was put there by the same people that put all of our power in a box, locked it away in the dark and told us not to open that box. *Do* open the mother-loving box, do enter, do create your own pathway, the one that leads to your remembered magic and creative power. Yes, that takes courage, but we are all so capable of cultivating it.

The courage to decide without certainty is not about having bulletproof confidence. It's about trust – not in the outcome, but in your capacity to meet whatever it is that comes your way. That's the shift. Instead of chasing guarantees, you build resilience. You're able to say: *Even if this choice leads me somewhere completely unexpected, I trust myself to navigate, to pivot and to begin all over again if needed.*

We can cultivate this courage by doing three things:

1. Listen to what's underneath the noise – the whisper from your big beat-y heart that says this feels real and true, even if it's terrifying.
2. Practise choosing in small ways – what to wear, who to text back, etc. – and notice how the world doesn't end when we follow our instincts. In fact, pay attention to all the ways life is brilliant when you do.
3. Forgive yourself quickly when you get it "wrong" – you *will* get it wrong!

We aren't here to be perfect; we're here to live and experience it all. The decisions and choices you make become portals and every time you walk through one without knowing what's on the other side, you honour your aliveness. *That's* courage.

The Power and Benefits of the Waxing Quarter Moon

The Waxing Quarter Moon is the phase of decision-making and disciplined devotion. It's where you take the dreams that you've planted and the ideas you've explored, and you make the choice – from the bottom of your big, beat-y heart – to commit to them.

This phase brings forward movement and determination and it's when you start to gain real traction in your creative process. It's where you're bold, decisive and forward-focused, and can feel and see the first tangible steps toward your vision coming to life.

This is a time to:

- ☽ Clarify your commitment to your creative process.
- ☽ Say yes to your vision and no to distractions.
- ☽ Take courageous action.

WAXING QUARTER MOON MAVEN

OCTAVIA E. BUTLER

(1947–2006)

"BE WHO YOU ARE AND NOT WHO SOMEONE ELSE WANTS YOU TO BE."
OCTAVIA E. BUTLER

Octavia E. Butler is a name that carries a *lot* of weight, not just because of *what* she created – she was the prolific author of over 15 fiction books, including *Parable of the Sower* and *Kindred*, which are both on my all-time favourite books list – but *how* she created them. Her journey from being a shy Black girl with dyslexia from Pasadena, USA to becoming a genre-defying, world-building literary powerhouse is an absolute mistress class in daring, declaring and showing up with relentless devotion to your craft.

Octavia had *no* interest in waiting for the world to be ready for her stories. She dared to write herself into a genre where no one like her had ever been seen before – science fiction, a space historically dominated by white men. She declared herself a writer before she had published a single book and she wrote, rewrote, and kept writing . . . And that, for me, is the magic of Octavia's legacy: she teaches us that creation is a practice of disciplined devotion, even when – especially when – the odds aren't stacked in your favour.

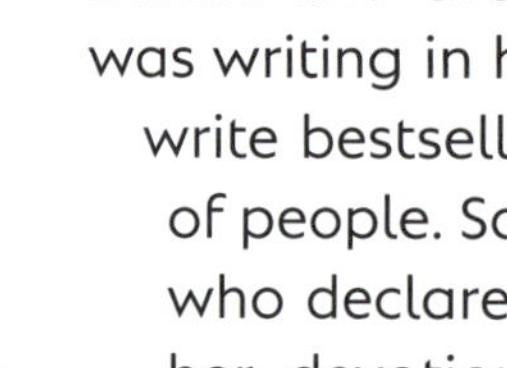

Before she ever saw her work on bookshelves, she was writing in her journal: "I am a bestselling writer. I write bestsellers. My books will be read by millions of people. So be it! See to it!" Now that is a woman who declared her vision and made it real through her devotion to the craft. This was manifesting *through* action. She got up early and showed up at her typewriter every single day; she worked menial jobs, committed to her stories, even when she faced rejection after rejection. Her devotion wasn't glamorous; it was gritty, it was showing up to write when no one believed in her or her vision yet.

Octavia knew the path wouldn't be easy and still she dared to write what wasn't being written. She didn't follow trends. She didn't water herself down to fit what the world expected. She declared: "This is the story I need to tell. This is the world I'm creating." She wove complex, flawed, magnificent Black women into her worlds and showed what it looked like to survive, adapt and transform – again and again.

And that's the energy of the Waxing Quarter Moon phase: the courage to take what's inside of you, show up with it, take action in a forward direction and bring it into form, even if it feels too big, too messy or too uncertain. That's how Octavia wrote masterpieces like *Kindred* and *Parable of the Sower* – books that are more relevant now than ever, which also make it super-clear that she wasn't just writing for her timeline; she was writing for our futures.

I adore Octavia E. Butler. She shows us what it looks like to hold a wild, tender vision and not flinch – I'm sure she experienced some self-doubt, but she knew that her creations, her voice and her stories mattered, and that it was up to her to dare to declare herself an author, one who is now considered "the mother of Afrofuturism" and whose visions remain relevant and critical in conversations about racial equity and social justice; an author who shapes myths from the margins and one who uses writing as a tool to respell reality.

So, when you're sitting with your doubts, wondering if your project is "good enough", wondering if *you* are good enough, channel Octavia. In the Waxing Quarter Moon, declare, show up and start. Take one small step, then another.

I am creating. I am devoted. So be it. See to it.

Because the magic in respelling your reality doesn't lie in waiting for the world to notice you and what it is that you're creating; the magic is in you daring to create, regardless.

What are you ready to commit to every single day?

Declare it *now*.

Write a personal "devotion statement" that names what you're building, who you're becoming and the daily and devotional practices that will make it happen.

The Hot Spots and Shadows of the Waxing Quarter Moon

With all its potential for progress, this Moon phase also brings friction and resistance. This is where your inner critic might start to make itself known (see page 168 for more on this). It's the phase where doubt, fear and self-sabotage can sneak in and try to convince you to quit before you've even begun.

We know that the Waxing Quarter Moon asks you to commit – to your creative process, to your ideas and to yourself. But this can, understandably, bring up fear. You might find yourself asking: *What if I fail? What if I'm not good enough? What if it's too hard?*

You might delay and/or avoid taking action, because you're scared of what's next. I get it - it's why I make the act of showing up daily a devotional one: I have talismanic jewellery that I put on when I start to create and that I take off when I've completed a writing session; I make an essential oil blend that corresponds with the energy of each book I write; and I make it as easeful as I possibly can to choose myself, so that commitment doesn't feel quite so heavy or overwhelming.

This phase can also bring up self-doubt and imposter syndrome. You've started making moves, but now you might hear that little voice in your head saying: *Who do I think I am? What if people find out I'm not good enough? Why bother when there are so many others doing this already?* And it's at this point you might feel tempted to quit or overthink the reality that you're respelling, but please know this: you, your voice, your art, your magic – they're *needed*. There's no one else who can create what you can in the way that you can.

And finally, the Waxing Quarter Moon is ultimately asking you to take your ideas one step further into the world, and this can feel vulnerable, especially for women who've been taught to stay small or not take up space. Fear of being seen and fear of judgement can cause you to hold back, but visibility is powerful. Being seen in your creative truth is revolutionary. It's OK to take the smallest of steps, but please, for the love of Octavia, *do take those steps.*

Mistress Your Magic

Here are some rituals and practices designed to help you become an energetic frequency match for your own magic and creative power during the Waxing Quarter Moon phase.

The One Brave Step Practice

To take one intentional, courageous step toward your creative dream.

You'll need

- Your journal or a notebook
- A timer

1. In your journal, write down one thing you've been avoiding in your creative process because of fear or doubt; for example: "starting the first chapter" or "sharing my work with someone I trust".
2. Set a timer for 20 minutes. Now take that one brave step during those 20 minutes. Don't overthink it. Just start. Whether it's writing the first sentence, or sending the email – do the thing.
3. When the timer sounds, reflect on how it felt to take action, even if it wasn't perfect.
4. In your journal, write:

I am showing up for my magic and creative power. I am being the creatrix I'm here to be.

The Burn the Doubt Practice

To release doubts, fears and resistance that may be holding you back from fully committing to your creative process.

You'll need

- A small fireproof bowl or a safe outdoor space
- A piece of paper
- A pen
- Matches or a lighter

1. Write down any fears, doubts or negative thoughts that are coming up for you. Be honest, don't hold back, let it all out; for example: *What if I'm not good enough? What if I fail? Who am I to do this?*

2. Take a deep breath in and hold for two seconds, then exhale long and audibly. Now take the paper and say out loud:

   I see these doubts and they do not define me, my magic or my creative power.

3. Burn the paper safely, watching the smoke rise. As it burns, visualize your doubts turning to ash and your creative power growing stronger.

4. Once the paper is fully burned, say:

   I release my fear. I choose courage. I am devoted to my creative process.

5. When I do this practice I offer the ashes to the elements, so either flush them, if you live near a body of water, release them there or give them to the Earth.

The Dare and Declare Ritual

To strengthen your commitment to your creative vision and declare it out loud.

You'll need

- A candle (preferably red, orange or gold for courage and confidence)
- Your journal or a piece of paper
- A pen
- *Optional*: a piece of jewellery or a charm to wear as a daily reminder of your commitment

1. Sit in a quiet space and light your candle. Take a moment to reflect on your creative dream, project and/or life choice.
2. In your journal, write a declaration of what it is that you're creating. Be bold, brave and specific; for example: "I am creating a collection of poetry that speaks my truth."
3. Place your hand over your heart and read your declaration out loud. Feel the energy of your words. Imagine them rippling out across lifetimes and timelines, out into the quantum field where the ancestors past and future are wanting and waiting to support you as the quantum field rearranges itself in order to support you.
4. If you have a charm or piece of jewellery, hold it and say:

   This is my symbol of devotion to my creative magic. I dare to show up. I declare my commitment to this process.

5. Blow out the candle, then wear your chosen symbol whenever you need a reminder of your power and commitment.

WAXING QUARTER MOON: THE DISRUPT

Action · Courage · Rewriting Patterns

The Science: This is where "tension" becomes a test. Old timelines will try to reassert themselves, but when you act from your unique-to-you frequency, you disrupt the Newtonian perception of reality and you let your *state* shape *your* reality.

The Magic: There will probably still be a part of you that needs to see it before you believe it, but when you interrupt the old pattern by taking action *before* you've got proof, you challenge the default settings, and the potential to change the outcome becomes much higher.

The Respell: Choose one bold, creative action: publish, pitch, post or perform something that defies your past self's limits, so that you're creating from your future and *not* your fear.

If you're a woman creating your own art and rewriting your reality, this Moon phase is a fierce and fertile ally – and this is the decision point. This is where you stop playing small and declare it. Claim it. Speak it into existence. Self-creation becomes real when you dare to tell the world – and yourself – what you're here to make, create and conjure and take devoted action.

It's in this phase that you shift from inner vision to outer expression, and it calls you to take the next step before you feel fully ready, knowing that readiness isn't a prerequisite for power, but movement definitely is. This Moon phase is where we learn that momentum isn't about speed; it's about choosing to keep going even when it's awkward, even when your inner critic is loud, even when nothing is guaranteed.

You keep moving, you keep showing up and you stop waiting to be discovered or rescued or validated and choose to initiate and respell your own next chapter. Your identity, your voice, your path – this Moon supports you in anchoring those through aligned action, by taking brave steps from a place of self-trust. This is the phase where you choose yourself, not once, but every single day. This is where you tell yourself:

I declare my desires boldly and move
with devotion toward them.
I choose my magic, I claim my path,
I move with steady devotion.

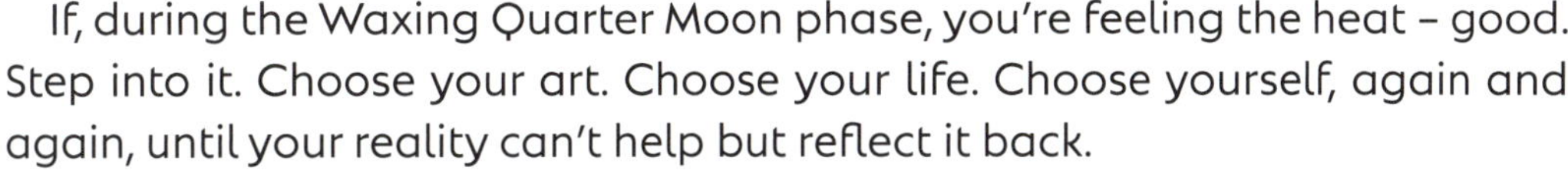

If, during the Waxing Quarter Moon phase, you're feeling the heat – good. Step into it. Choose your art. Choose your life. Choose yourself, again and again, until your reality can't help but reflect it back.

WAXING GIBBOUS MOON

BE YOUR OWN MUSE

MAKE OUT WITH YOURSELF.
MUSS UP THE SHEETS. WITH INK, POETRY, PAINT – ALL OF LIFE.

In the Waxing Gibbous Moon phase, fall in love with the process of creating and allow yourself to be in the flow, *your* flow. Create the necessary conditions for you and your art to bear the juiciest fruit.

Waxing Gibbous Moon Energy and How It Affects You

You're not quite at the fullness of the Moon, but the energy is continuing to rise and the momentum of the Waxing Quarter Moon – the get-shit-done energy that got activated in the last phase – is still very much at play here, which means you're able to be fully immersed in the act and art of creation.

In the creative process, the Waxing Gibbous Moon phase is where your idea has shape, your art has form, and now you're sculpting the details.

WAXING GIBBOUS MOON

- Celebrate your progress so far – name your wins.
- Stand in your creative space and own it.
- Affirm your creative worthiness daily.
- Treat your creative practice as sacred.
- Trust the flow.
- Experience heightened passion.
- Recognize beauty.
- Modify and tweak your idea/energy/way of being so that it's as effective as possible.
- Weed out anything that's stopping your idea from blossoming.

Sounds: Moody, empowering alt-pop or indie rock. Think: Banks, CMAT, Halsey.

Essential oils and herbs: Frankincense (self-reflection and empowerment), jasmine (self-worth).

Extra-sensory anchor: Wear something that makes you feel iconic, even if no one sees it but you.

This is the polishing phase – but don't confuse that with perfectionism. This isn't about nit-picking or second-guessing yourself; it's about honouring what you're creating by giving it your full presence, your full heart, your full attention. It's honouring your commitment – not just to the project, but to the version of you who dared to begin.

It's in this phase that you can fine-tune your energy. You can elevate your environment and show yourself that you're someone who follows through, especially when you're at the edge of "almost". You can start a conversation with the work and yourself as its creatrix: you can look to understand it (and yourself), analyse it (and yourself) and ask questions of it (and yourself):

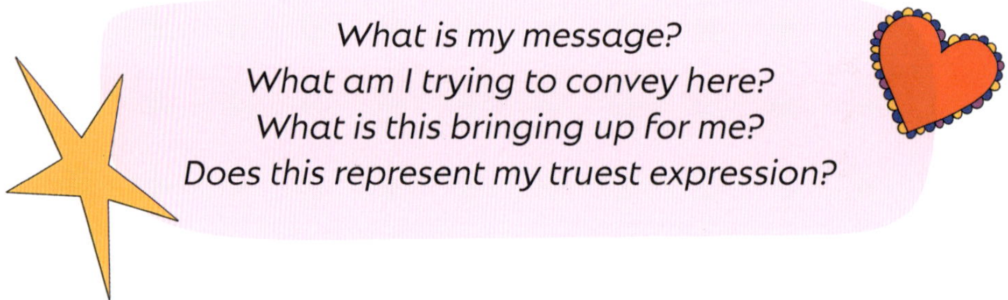

You can do a little light pruning of weeds here, not a full edit, but if there are some things that just don't make sense, in both the work and yourself, don't be afraid to cut them loose to protect what's blossoming.

This phase is like the end of spring and beginning of summer, so take a moment to contemplate the growth of your dream. Check in with the conditions of your personal "soil". Sometimes we have a tendency to get so passionate and creative with the *doing* that the needs and nourishment – which we highlighted as necessary back at the Waxing Crescent Moon – can sometimes get pushed aside; so make sure that your "soil" remains fecund!

Be in collaboration and union with yourself as your muse, make out together and recognize that it's here, in this final growth stage of the cycle, that we can really get to know our work/idea, refine it and align with it.

The Waxing Gibbous Moon phase asks you to fall in love with the process; you're sculpting the self who can hold the fullness that's coming. That's what makes your magic sustainable.

Waxing Gibbous Moon: A Riff

I used to hate being "in process". I'm very impatient by nature, but now, it's all that I'm interested in. I used to hate being seen; then I wrote books, people read them and now really intimate stuff about my lived experience lives in the pages of those books for anyone to access. It's all thoroughly contradictory, and it's in the Waxing Gibbous Moon phase that we find these things out about ourselves, as we get to know ourselves as the one who is a creatrix.

There was a time, quite soon after both my parents died, when I was all about fierce truth; I shared everything in real time and I desperately wanted everyone else to show up with their heart bleeding in their hands too. I wasn't interested in anything except the in-the-moment truth. In retrospect, I think you only ever show up that way when you have nothing to lose.

My parents had died and I really did have nothing else to lose. Then I wrote a book called *Witch* and because of a tight writing deadline, I didn't have chance to show it to anyone else before it came out. I shared some pretty big parts of me in there and, jeez, I really felt the impact – physically, mentally, emotionally – of sharing it directly with the world without having been soothed, held and witnessed during the book's creation. It left me feeling like a walking,talking, open and exposed wound, which is why I now create circles and containers for that process. Women *need* spaces to share and create in, to nurture and tend to their ideas as they come to fruition.

Ideas, art, dreams, books – lives even – do *not* come fully formed; sometimes they start out as something else entirely. But if that idea or dream is loved on, if it's tended to and nurtured, it can blossom and bloom into something quite incredible. However, it needs time to grow. It needs patience to see what it will become and in the process you need to practise being seen.

In what may seem like a totally contradictory statement, we also can't wait until we have it all figured out and ready to share, either. If part of the story we tell ourselves is that it isn't OK to share unless we have our shit together, we may start to hoard everything until it's nice and neat, and then we *might* consider sharing, but for the most part we never actually do.

The uncomfortable moments of sharing when we're vulnerable and we don't have everything sorted out are important. They're moments of true intimacy. But heads up; not everyone is worthy of reading our rough drafts, or hearing about our big dreams, and not everyone will treat them gently and respectfully, so I beg of you not to share your ideas with just anyone. (From personal experience, if you're writing a book, don't ask your best friend's opinion unless your best friend is your potential target audience, as they, and you, will have to navigate the truth, your friendship, feelings *and* emotions when giving and receiving feedback!)

The idea of being seen can be debilitating, so when in the "process", and especially in this Waxing Gibbous Moon Phase, don't be too quick to share everything with the world. Let ideas be tended to and loved on so they can develop. BUT – and this is a big BUT – don't wait until it's "finished" either.

Let yourself and your shitty first drafts, your in-process dreams, be seen in a state of imperfection and incompletion by those with whom it feels safe and good to share, so that you get to experience vulnerability safely. You get to see where you might be triggered and where the pain and discomfort sit in your body, so that when you *do* share your magic/story/truth with the world, you will feel anchored and powerful. Roarrrrrr!

What does the idea of "being seen" evoke in you?

Be Your Own Muse

When you become your own muse, you stop being someone else's project and start being your own mother-loving masterpiece. Women have always been painted, adored, possessed and written about – but rarely given the pen, the brush or the microphone to create their own reality. The muse, traditionally, was silent. Beautiful. Observed. Objectified. So, when you decide to be your own muse, you reclaim your power to create, embody and initiate.

You turn your creative gaze back to yourself. You're no longer waiting to be seen, chosen or approved of, because you choose yourself. You recognize your own rhythm, your own hunger, your own holy contradictions – and most importantly, you don't apologize for them.

In a culture that actively profits from our self-doubt and self-editing, to be your own muse – to believe that *your* life, *your* truth, your way of seeing the world are worthy of devotion – is revolutionary. It's subversive (and really bloody brilliant) to say: *I am inspired by me. I am moved by my own magic.*

You, as your own muse, is the part of you that is able to shrug off fear, expectation, worry and doubt and is just in love with the act (and art) of creating. *Sigh*. You, as your own muse, soothe yourself, enthuse yourself, tend to the fire and bring yourself to a place of joy and pleasure through creation.

I invite you to meet and make out with yourself as muse. Ask yourself, as your own muse, questions such as:

Muse, what do you love?
What are your favourite colours? Flavours?
Textures?
What are your favourite smells?
What is your favourite way for us to date and create together?

Really get to know her, enter into a relationship with her, create an image of her and frame it; kiss it or give it a wink every time you pass it.

Me, as my own muse, has elements of every Moon Maven described in *Respell Your Reality*, as well as Anaïs Nin, Joan Jett, Björk, Mary Magdalene, Miriam Margolyes, Boudicca, Jem (from *Jem and the Holograms*) and She-Ra (from *She-Ra: Princess of Power*). She smokes, she's smart, she's funny, she's seductive and sensual (men and women and those without gender labels *all* find her attractive) and she calls me into the deepest part of myself when daring me to create. She does not fuck around.

She loves the smell of jasmine, ylang-ylang, rose and amber, so to evoke her and flirt with her, I make sure I have these smells in my workspace.

When we become our own muse, we change the narrative for everyone else. We stop telling the boring,snoring, old-paradigm story that beauty, brilliance and magic live outside of us and, instead, we model a new mythology – one where inspiration is cyclical, messy, sensual and self-sourced. We make art from the inside out, we create lives with lines of poetry and we become impossible to domesticate.

So please, please, please *be your own muse*. Not just for your creativity, but for your wholeness. For the way you walk through the world. For other women who will learn that the muse isn't an idea outside of them; it's self-initiation and self-creation and it's how you rewrite reality with your own hands, on your own terms, in your own most exquisite image.

The Power and Benefits of the Waxing Gibbous Moon

The Waxing Gibbous Moon is a phase of editing, fine-tuning and elevating. I won't lie, this phase used to make me wildly uncomfortable – the pressure, the weight of what's unfinished, the sharp voice of perfectionism creeping in at the edges, whispering: *It's not good enough. It's not ready.* Maybe we're not ready. But we're learning the Moon's language now.

This phase is actually a forge. It's the place where your ideas get tempered by fire and where your art and life sharpens into something more truthful, more you. The friction that you inevitably experience (please say it's not just me?!) is a signal that suggests something important is happening here. So instead of rushing to completion, pause. Let your hands, mind and heart work together to refine what's happening *in* the process. Ask:

What am I really trying to say here?
What does it need from me to really come alive?

And here's the magic that I've discovered: it's not just my creative process that becomes more whole in this phase, it's me. As you shape your art, you shape yourself.

As you refine your project, you refine your purpose. And with every decision, every adjustment, every moment of showing up for your process, you expand into more of the woman that you're here to be.

Yes, the fear of being seen may bubble up here. The fear of finishing. Of stepping out of the shadows and saying: *Here. This is me. This is my truth.*

Yet, the Waxing Gibbous Moon teaches us to honour those edges, to embrace the tension between almost and arrival. It teaches us that we don't have to force fullness; we just have to tend to the flame and trust the process.

WAXING GIBBOUS MOON MAVEN

FRIDA KAHLO

(1907–1954)

"I AM MY OWN MUSE. I AM THE SUBJECT I KNOW BEST. THE SUBJECT I WANT TO BETTER."

FRIDA KAHLO

I *love* Frida Kahlo. She really lived her art. Through pain, through passion and the most unimaginable odds, she painted herself into existence.

Born in 1907 in Coyoacán, Mexico, Frida's life was shaped early on by suffering. At the age of six, she contracted polio, which left her with a limp. At 18, she was in a horrific bus accident that shattered her body, breaking her spine, pelvis and leg, and which left her in chronic pain for the rest of her life. She began painting while bedridden in a body cast, using a mirror above her bed to observe herself. That mirror – and the gaze it invited – became a way for Frida to paint and adorn her pain and to make it powerful.

She became her own muse because she had to. The outside world didn't reflect her experience – so she created her own reality.

Long before front-facing cameras and ring lights, Frida was using mirrors and paintbrushes to document her evolving identity. In fact, some might say that Frida Kahlo was the mother of "the selfie", not in the TikTok, filtered, curated-for-approval kind of way, but in the OG, raw, revolutionary sense of the word. She painted nearly 55 self-portraits, which were never about vanity (although there would be nothing wrong with that if they were); they were about her visibility. She was telling the world: *This is how I see myself. This is my truth. This is my body, my pain, my power, my story.* And yes, Frida did paint her pain, but she also painted her power, her politics, her love affairs, her heritage, her body, her identity.

She posed herself in pain, in longing, in rage, in eroticism, in defiance – and then she magnified it. Her unibrow and moustache were never edited out; they were accentuated. Her corsets and surgical scars were adorned, stylized and painted with doves and flames. She took her physical reality – damaged spine, interrupted fertility, political heartbreak – and turned it into a visual autobiography, using her work to interrogate, explore and express herself and blurring the line between art and life, truth and dream, body and soul.

Her brows, her clothes, her gaze – everything about her was a conscious act of self-authorship and she used her appearance to make a statement. She played with gender. She fused traditional Tehuana dress with surrealist self-portraiture and made herself iconic by being herself fully, no filter, no compromise.

The Waxing Gibbous is the almost Full Moon, the moment of tight creative stretch. You can feel the weight of what you're building. You see the shape of it taking form, but it's not quite there yet. There's pressure. There's friction. There's a wild heartbeat that asks: *Can you hold your nerve? Can you keep going?*

Frida did.

Her life was a constant dance with this tension and she kept creating. She didn't wait for perfect health, perfect circumstances or perfect timing; she painted through her injuries, alchemized her heartbreak into beauty, took fragments of her life and turned them into fierce, vivid expressions of selfhood – and she didn't hide. Even when her work was considered "too intimate" or "too raw", she shared it with the world. She trusted that her truth had value. She trusted that even if her body was broken, her spirit and her art were alive, vibrant and worthy of being seen.

That's the Waxing Gibbous Moon's invitation: trust yourself. Trust your process. Stand in the tension and let it make you stronger. Let it sharpen your edges. Let it bring you closer to the fullest version of your art, your story and yourself.

When you feel the pull of perfectionism, the ache of nearly-there, channel Frida. Because like her, you are both the art and the artist.

The Hot Spots and Shadows of the Waxing Gibbous Moon

From personal experience, the Waxing Gibbous Moon phase is where I feel the most pressure to be perfect. I'm in it, that almost-there state creates necessary tension – and it's where, usually in a very dramatic fashion, I'll want to abandon it all. Remember: perfection is a thief of progress. Or . . . if I don't want to abandon it all, I'll just want it *done*. In the wise words of Natasha Bedingfield, it's here that you're "so close, you can almost taste it", but rushing will risk compromising your vision. Trust the timing. Let things unfold at your right rhythm.

As we edge closer to the Full Moon, it's inevitable that fear of being seen might arise – after all, the Full Moon illuminates everything, so that feeling is only natural. Yet I've found that witnessing it and naming it weakens its hold. Lean into rhythms and rituals to stay anchored in your truth, self-trust and your reason.

Each morning, place your hand on your heart and declare:

I TRUST MY PROCESS. I TRUST MY PACE. I TRUST MY POWER.

Mistress Your Magic

Here are some rituals and practices designed to help you become an energetic frequency match for your own magic and creative power during the Waxing Gibbous Moon phase.

The Fuck Perfection Ritual

To break free from the grip of perfectionism and root yourself in daily devotion to your creative process.

You'll need

- A candle (gold or white for illumination and clarity)
- Your current work in progress
- A timer
- Your journal or a piece of paper
- A pen

1. Light your candle in a safe place and set a timer for 20 to 30 minutes. During this time, engage directly with your creative work. Edit a piece. Shape an idea. Refine one element of your project. Don't aim to finish – just aim to be present, without any distractions.
2. When the timer ends, journal for five minutes on the following:
   - What did I enjoy in this session?
   - What is evolving in my work and myself?
3. Blow out your candle, sealing your practice in trust.
4. I like to do this ritual as often as I can, especially during the Waxing Gibbous Moon phase, as it shifts your energy from chasing an elusive "perfect" outcome to anchoring in steady, loving attention to your craft and your growth.

The "I Am Worthy of Being Seen" Ritual

A practice to honour yourself as a mirror, a muse and a myth.

You'll need

- A mirror
- A song or playlist of choice
- An essential oil/scent of choice
- Your journal or a piece of paper
- A pen

1. Set up a mirror (the size doesn't matter!). Not to judge or critique yourself, but to witness.
2. Anchor yourself by saying this invocation aloud:

   I am here to meet myself as art.

3. Gaze into the mirror. Don't pose. Don't perform. Just hold your own gaze. What arises? Let it come. An emotion? Resistance? Admiration?
4. Now ask:

   What parts of me are asking to be seen?
   Where am I hiding?
   If I were painting myself tonight,
   what colours would I choose? Why?

5. Play your song as you write or draw your responses. Dance if your body takes over. Let your self-exploration become a performance.
6. Anoint yourself with a diluted essential oil or scent. Look at yourself in the mirror, touch your heart space with your hand and tell yourself:

   I do not need to be understood to be real.

7. Leave a mark in your journal or a physical offering on your altar to symbolize what was revealed (it might be a petal, a word, etc.) and let your next creation be shaped by this truth.

Get Full Moon-Ready

To physically embody the feeling of what it means to be full and whole and to energize your nervous system for visibility and expansion.

You'll need

- A playlist that makes you feel unapologetically alive
- Space to move

1. Press play on your playlist and let yourself move as if whatever you're here to create is already in the world, is already celebrated, is already complete.
2. Experience the energy of what that feels like pulsing through your body. Stretch, sway, dance, or even just breathe deeply into the feeling of readiness. Do this for as long as feels good.
3. Yep, that's it, we really don't need to complicate this. Your body is your most creative tool and when you embody the energy of readiness, you create a powerful internal alignment with your external reality. This primes your nervous system for expansion and visibility.

WAXING GIBBOUS MOON

Clean-Up · Belief Work · Precision

The Science: Your beliefs, emotions and habits all shape the frequency you emit. That frequency interacts with the field, whether you're aware of it or not. If you keep focusing on old stories or patterns, you reinforce them. In quantum terms, waves of possibility collapse into form when observed with clarity and emotional alignment. So, if you want to respell your reality, start by noticing where your attention is still locked on to a version of you that no longer fits.

The Magic: This phase holds the magic of energetic calibration. Doubt sends mixed signals, but belief rings clear and the field listens. What you feel becomes your frequency, and your frequency shapes what shows up. You're not just imagining it, you're instructing reality with your resonance.

The Respell: Refine your broadcast by tidying up the stray frequencies of fear, impatience or sabotage. What are you still observing that you don't want to create? Clear the clutter and sharpen your signal.

When you see yourself as worthy of your own creation, everything changes. Self-recognition and becoming your own muse are the power moves of the Waxing Gibbous Moon phase that support this. This phase is where you take yourself and your capacity as a creatrix seriously: you honour the process and trust yourself (and the stretch) to spell-shift your life and all that it is you create.

This is a phase of fine-tuning your spell. Aligning and refining your magic and witnessing and recognizing yourself as the woman who commits to what she starts. You're no longer casting wild what-ifs into the quantum field – you're shaping them with your own hands and heart and gaining crystal-clear clarity in the process, so that you can polish, adjust and elevate your work (and yourself) into its full expression. This is the Moon phase when you become the living proof of your devotion.

Take what it is you're creating – a project, yourself, your life, your reality – and see it through the eyes of love and care. This isn't about criticizing or tearing it down; it's about lovingly shaping it into the most truthful, beautiful expression it can be. And that tension you're probably feeling? Know that it's expanding you. It's your art, yourself, growing bigger than it's ever been. Let it stretch you. This is where you grow, this is where you embody it before it's real, and become the energetic and vibrational match for its arrival.

The Waxing Gibbous Moon reminds us that you, your art and magic are really bloody alive and every brushstroke, every word written, every decision you make marks both the creation of your work and the creation of yourself in a reality that you choose. The spell is in motion – keep going.

FULL MOON

INNOVATE. BE SEEN. EXPRESS YOURSELF.

EXPRESS YOURSELF.
SHINE.
BE SEEN AS THE POWERFUL AND POTENT CREATRIX THAT YOU ARE.
DARE TO BE CELEBRATED.
DANCE, SING, WRITE YOUR REALITY IN YOUR FULLEST EXPRESSION.

Don't hide your light: let yourself and your work take centre stage in the spotlight of the Full Moon and dare to be witnessed.

FULL MOON

- Be seen.
- Host a solo celebration for how far you've come.
- Let your voice be heard – sing, speak, write and share.
- Acknowledge your progress: name every win, big and small.
- Bask in your own brilliance.

Sounds: A celebration playlist! Think: Stevie Nicks, Dua Lipa, Haim.

Essential oils and herbs: Ylang-ylang (sensual expression), bergamot (confidence).

Extra-sensory anchor: Candlelight, fairy lights and a mirror ball: bright and alive, and with the mirror ball to reflect your own creative shine.

Full Moon Energy and How It Affects You

When the Moon is opposite the Sun and fully illuminated, art, creativity and intentions are made manifest. Like the Sun at the summer solstice, this is where the Moon energy reaches its peak.

This is the Moon of full and maximum expansion, and a time for your most outward expression. This is a phase to be seen and to socialize and to share yourself and your work with the world, because the energy here is amplified, illuminated and heightened. Oftentimes, introverts or those who are sensitive can find a Full Moon *really hard* because it can feel like you're feeling . . . everything. In the same way that those who are sensitive to rising oestrogen find ovulation a really tricky time in the menstrual cycle, lots of us feel like we need to wear shades at the Full Moon, too. Because the energy? It's intense. However, others thrive here. Feel into which one *you* are.

This phase is the heat of summer, energy is high and *everything* is exposed. (I've often described this phase as feeling like someone has posted a photo of me nude to a million strangers, while other women I've worked with come fully alive here – I've found it really is person-dependent more than any other phase.)

The Full Moon can, and for the most part does, reflect back to you the reality of your New Moon intentions, dreams and visions. You'll discover if those modifications you made in the last phase have actually made sense and feel good, and you'll see what your original vision has now become and where it's going.

The Full Moon: A Riff

The Full Moon is all about exposure and yes, it is intense. If, like me, you're a creative woman, especially one who's been burned by visibility or made to feel smaller by scrutiny, a freak-out in this phase is completely understandable, because its invitation to be seen can definitely feel more like a demand and a command. The good news is that I've also experienced the most beautiful paradox: the Full Moon isn't just about being exposed; it's also about being illuminated. And illumination is powerful, not just so that others can see you, but so that you can see yourself.

At its core, the Full Moon is a creative climax, bringing whatever it is that you've been building, creating and respelling during the waxing phases into full view. If you've been creating something like a piece of writing, a visual work, a project, or even a new version of yourself, then this is when it really gets to be seen. And that can feel terrifying, because everything is amplified here: excitement, emotion, doubt, desire – *all of it*. It turns up the volume on your creative energy and your inner critic in equal measure.

The trick is to treat that spotlight like a pull-back-the-curtain-and-reveal moment: you get to see what's working, what's not, what's ready to be shared and what's still ripening. I've found it helpful to remember that I always get to choose what I share, what I release and what I hold close, and that being seen doesn't mean being stripped bare; you're allowed some mystery. (In fact, I would actively encourage that, although that could be due to the amount of Scorpio I have in my natal astrological chart!)

However, the biggest gift of the Full Moon in my own experience is that it's here that you're shown what's already inside you, albeit magnified. And, yes, sometimes seeing your own power clearly can be the scariest thing of all, and yet . . . this is also where your most magnetic art, creations, life and lived experiences are waiting and wanting to be fully expressed.

Being Full of Yourself

When the Moon is at her fullest, she's lit, fully visible and showing up in her entirety, so this is the time to practise being unapologetically, wildly, gloriously full of yourself. Know this: your fullness isn't a threat, it's a frequency. It calls your people to you. It shows others what's possible when a woman decides to be self-sourced, both *in* her power and *in* her body; because if you're not full of you, then what fills the space? Other people's opinions? Old programming? Cultural noise? There's no room for other people's projections in a body that's full of self-trust, creative fire and inner knowing.

When you're full of yourself – charged, rooted, aligned and lit up – you're magnetic. Look at the Moon: she doesn't technically *do* anything, she just is. And yet she pulls tides, stirs blood, lights up the night sky, inspires countless songs and poems, and has wolves (and on the odd occasion, me) howling at her, because that is the essence of feminine magnetism: presence to her wholeness. She knows herself in all her phases and it's this energy that attracts, because it's whole. (It's wholly holy.)

And as for you, your creativity and magic, respelling realities from this place and space? Electrifying.

When you're full all the way up with your own essence – your desires, your voice, your vision – you become a gravitational field. The right ideas, people, opportunities, collaborators, lovers, readers, fellow life-experiencers . . . they feel your pulse, they sense the coherence and

they lean in, because you're not leaking energy or second-guessing yourself. You're anchored and you're whole.

Your art, your words, your work – *you* – become irresistible, because they carry a frequency of truth, of embodiment, of "this is me, take it or leave it". And that kind of energy is captivating because it's really bloody rare. It's not needy, it's not asking for approval; it's self-ownership and it's glorious!

This is why my call to action is this: we need a full-blown renaissance of women being deliciously, daringly, divinely full of themselves.

Full of our ideas.

Full of our contradictions.

Full of our sensuality, our genius, our mess, our magic.

Full of everything we've been told to tone down, smooth over and/or hide.

Because when we are full of ourselves, we're not waiting to be filled by anyone else's version of who we should be. We stop using our magic power of shape-shifting to meet the approval of others, we stop leaking power and we stop editing our brilliance to make others more comfortable.

So let's reclaim it, shall we?

Let's wear it like the most deliciously decadent perfume.

Let's toast to it under the Full Moon.

Let's make it the standard, not the exception.

The world needs women who dare to take up space in the shape of their own creation.

The Power and Benefits of the Full Moon

When the Moon is full, we have reached the height of our forward push, and our creative energy is also at its peak here. (I speak in broad brushstrokes: this might not be true for you, and it's your job to get curious about all the feelings and expressions at play throughout each of the phases, so you can really start to crack your own creatrix code and respell *your* reality.)

It's a phase that shines light on your progress, your achievements and your growth. It lets you see what you've created and who you've become in the process.

Another plus? The Full Moon is relational. It highlights connection, resonance and reflection, making this a great time to collaborate, to host and to share. Let others see you in your element. Let your creativity connect. That's what the Moon is doing – reflecting the light of the Sun – and there's magic in that.

FULL MOON MAVEN

VALI MYERS
(1930–2003)

"EVEN WHEN I WAS YOUNG, I LIVED IN A WORLD OF MY OWN MAKING."
VALI MYERS

Vali Myers lived her entire life like the Full Moon phase: bold, bright and fully lit up by love, art and magic.

Born in Sydney in 1930, Vali was a wild child from the start. She'd skip school to draw, dancing barefoot and refusing to be tamed by convention. By the age of 14, she had left home; by 19, she was in post-war Paris, living on the streets of the Left Bank, dancing for tips and being photographed by the Dutch photographer Ed van der Elsken, who immortalized her in his book *Love on the Left Bank*.

But Vali was no passive muse. (You'd expect nothing less, would you?!) She was a creatrix of worlds. Her intricate, hallucinatory drawings – some crafted with crow-quill pens, Chinese ink and gold leaf – were Alice-in-Wonderland style rabbit holes into her inner cosmos that were filled with foxes, owls, wild women and mythic beasts. She often worked by candlelight, in solitude, sometimes taking years to complete a single piece. Her art was deeply personal, frequently reflecting her own experiences and emotions.

Visually, Vali was unforgettable; a flame-haired enchantress with fierce kohl-rimmed eyes, a tattooed face and sharp cheekbones. Her appearance was equal parts witch, dancer, animal and queen. She tattooed her face with a moustache and decorative dots across her cheeks long before facial tattoos were remotely acceptable for women in the West. She claimed her face as part of her art, turning herself into a living magical sigil.

Her hair – long and red and often plaited or left wild – was her crown. She wore layers of embroidered skirts, scarves, silver jewellery, talismans and handmade clothes, and she looked like no one else because she didn't want to be anyone else.

Her entire life was her canvas and her diary pages are splashed with wild, swirling sketches and fierce words that read like spells. The remote valley in Italy that she called home for over 40 years was as much a work of art as her drawings – lush, overgrown, full of foxes and owls and raw beauty. It was like stepping into a painting no one had ever finished. No electricity, no running water and also, more importantly, no need to explain herself. (Although people definitely demanded she try.)

She was creating and respelling her reality living at the edge of worlds – in the liminal spaces between nature and art – and her presence was intoxicating, because she was the full embodiment of creative freedom.

This is the essence of the Full Moon phase. Vali shows us what it looks like when a woman refuses to dim her light. When she chooses her own creative sovereignty over conformity. When she lets her passion pulse through every choice, every creation, every wild-eyed step she makes and takes.

In the Full Moon phase, Vali Myers shows us that life can be your greatest work of art. That your body is a canvas, your home a temple, your choices a spell; and that to be full of yourself is to turn your whole life into a love letter to your truth and reality creation.

If Frida painted the raw self, Vali became it. Fierce. Feral and free.

The Hot Spots and Shadows of the Full Moon

As I mentioned previously, the Full Moon energy is big, sometimes too big, and you might feel wired, overstimulated or scattered by the intensity of it. (I do!) If you're sensitive to energy, slow down, ground yourself and try to stay present in the moment, because the Full Moon will amplify emotions. Joy, grief, pride, frustration – all of the feels can and will show up here, so allow them to be present, and either let them move through you, shaking your body regularly, Taylor Swift style, or use them as creative fuel. Just don't keep them bottled up.

There's also what I call "completion pressure", when you might feel pressured to finish and complete everything *right now*. It's OK to still be in progress and, spoiler alert: we're always in progress. My advice? Honour what's complete and trust what's still unfolding, because you being real and true will always shine brighter than being perfect or finished.

Mistress Your Magic

On the next page you'll find rituals and practices designed to help you become an energetic frequency match for your magic and creative power during the Full Moon.

The Full Moon Art Date

This is an opportunity, under the Full Moon, to witness all that's being illuminated and turn it into art.

You'll need

- Art supplies
- A locale of your choice (it could be a bed picnic, a coffee shop date, a trip to the sea – your choice)
- A big open heart

1. When you are settled in your chosen spot with your art supplies, ask yourself:

   If I fully claimed my life as my art, what would I dare to express, create, or share today?

2. Let your thoughts on this be an uncensored, full-hearted spill onto the page, using your art materials to illustrate your answers:
   - What truth, idea or creation is burning inside you, ready to be seen?
   - Where have you been dimming your fire, and how can you fan the flames instead?
   - If you stopped waiting for perfection, applause or permission, what bold step would you take right now?
   - How would you move, dress, speak and create if you truly believed, in Vali Myers style, "I am the art"?
3. End your Full Moon art date with a simple declaration, written in bold letters across the page:

   I am art.

4. Let this become something you do each and every Full Moon to honour yourself and honour the process.

The Shine and Share Boldly Ritual

To energetically align with visibility and joyful self-expression.

You'll need

- A candle (white or gold for radiance)
- A piece of your creative work (finished or in progress)
- A mirror or open window (for reflection and projection)

1. Light your candle and say aloud:

   I am ready to be seen.

2. Hold your creative work in your hands. Look at it with pride, whether it feels finished or not.
3. Stand in front of the mirror or window and read an excerpt aloud, or simply speak about your creation as if you are sharing it with an audience who is thrilled to receive it. Feel what it's like to speak with pride about something you've created.
4. Tap your heart gently three times and let this feeling land in your body.
5. Close by saying aloud:

   I honour my creative power and allow it to be seen and celebrated.

6. Blow out the candle to seal the ritual.
7. *Optional extra:* Share a piece of your work with your community under the Full Moon, whether it's on social media or with a friend: let yourself witness that you can hold the energy of visibility.

Moon Bathing for Magnetic Energy Practice

To physically absorb the lunar radiance and charge your creative field with expansion.

You'll need

- Access to moonlight (e.g., a window, balcony, garden, or open sky)
- Your journal or piece of paper
- A pen

1. Stand, sit or lie under the Moon. If you can't see the Moon, trust that her energy is still able to reach you.
2. Close your eyes and visualize the Moon's light pouring over you, filling every cell of your body and being with warmth and activating your creative power.
3. Breathe deeply and let the light of the Moon move into your heart, your hands and your creative centre.
4. After 5–10 minutes, open your journal and write:

   What is ready to be expressed through me?

5. Let your answers flow onto the page.
6. Close by placing your hands on your heart and whispering:

   I am a radiant vessel of creative power.
   I receive, I create, I magnetize.

FULL MOON: POSSIBILITY BECOMES MATTER

Illumination · Visibility · Amplification

The Science: At the quantum level, the act of observation collapses the wave. What you've been focusing on – what you've emotionally charged and repeatedly observed – now crystalizes into form. This is cause and effect reversed: not "I see it, so I believe it", but "I believed it, so now I see it".

The Magic: The field has responded. What you've magnetized through emotion, attention and intention becomes visible now – whether aligned or not. Remember, though, that the Full Moon is simply a mirror; it's not a final verdict. Its magic is in clarity and amplification: you're being shown what you've been transmitting, consciously or not.

The Respell: Stand in the mirror of your creation and witness it without flinching. Celebrate what's aligned and course-correct what's not. Let this moment illuminate the power of *your* frequency.

At the Full Moon, you reach your peak of creativity; things make sense, there's clarity, you can see what's working and what's not; you can articulate it, you can ride the creative wave and let your art, and your heart, take up space.

The power of the Full Moon is that it illuminates both your creations and the creatrix herself – *you*.

It casts light on what you've made, but also on who you've become through the making. It reminds you that you are the fire, the creation and the magic in motion that can and will respell reality.

WANING GIBBOUS MOON

DEFINE. REFINE. ALIGN. DISCERN.

CATCH YOUR BREATH, CREATRIX.
CELEBRATE HOW FAR YOU'VE COME AND
WHAT YOU'VE CREATED SO FAR.
NOW, CLOSE YOUR EYES.
USE THE POWER OF YOUR THIRD EYE,
YOUR INNER SIGHT AND VISION,
TO SEE WHAT REALLY NEEDS AND WANTS TO BE SEEN.

During the Waning Gibbous Moon phase, let your sensory system guide you in refining and aligning your vision with what truly matters, using the power of discernment – the art of honouring your creative clarity . . .

WANING GIBBOUS MOON

- Make a Keep/Refine/Release/Align list.
- Honour your natural slowing-down without guilt.
- Trust that discernment, alignment and refinement are wildly creative acts.
- Celebrate what feels aligned and alive.
- Activate your inner sight.

Sounds: Grounding but strong. Think: Lana Del Rey, Róisín Murphy, Ibeyi.

Essential oils and herbs: Cedarwood (clarity), eucalyptus (mental freshness).

Extra-sensory anchor: Tea or herbal infusions, something earthy to bring you into your body after the intensity of the Full Moon.

Waning Gibbous Moon Energy and How It Affects You

You expand and ascend to your fullest potential with the Waxing to Full Moon phases and now, as the Moon wanes, moving from full to dark, we are given the opportunity to release, to edit and to assess what's been manifested and illuminated at the fullness of the Moon.

FYI, this phase can feel a bit like a kick in the ovaries. Mainly because it's in this phase that you realize you're *not* Queen of Freakin' Everything. I know, *rude*, right? You can't do everything; I mean you can, of course you can, but you *will* break. This half of the cycle is a call to slow down the pace, stop being so outward-facing and to turn inward.

As the Moon begins its journey back toward the darkness, be in deep bows for what you've created and brought into being so far, honour your bounty, celebrate you and your ability to create.

The good news? While the can-do energy may be lower, in the second half of the cycle, your intuition and sensory system becomes heightened and more powerful – and that begins here, in the Waning Gibbous Moon phase. This phase gives us inner vision. It's here that you can look at your work, the way you create, a person or a situation, and see the puzzle pieces that are misplaced, that aren't in order, or are missing entirely. (Word of warning: it's here that we can sometimes come across as Judge Judy when we "share" what we see. Not everyone's ready to hear it. This and the next two phases are *amazing* for practising discernment when working out what needs to be shared and what doesn't with friends, fam and the collective.)

That inner vision activates wise discernment, helping us to choose what stays and what goes – what still feels true, and what needs reshaping, editing and extra attention so that you can shape and spell it into something sharper, more aligned, more you. The refinement process begins here, as you take the clarity you experienced in the Full Moon phase and align with what it is that you stand for and how you want to work and live in the world. You ensure that your energy, your projects and your priorities are all moving in the same direction and bring a real sense – through *your* senses – of coherence to your creativity and to your life.

This is a phase of saying yes with conviction and no with confidence. Of trusting that letting go of what doesn't serve your evolution is an act of devotion to your creative power and to yourself. It's about refining and aligning your energy and frequency accordingly to shape not only your work but your world and reality with precision and power.

The Waning Gibbous Moon: A Riff

I come from a traveller family, and all of the women in my matrilineal line had what was called "all-seeing sight". Now, this isn't something that only women in traveller communities have – I believe we *all* have access to it – it's just that in my fam, it was cultivated. Some would call us a seer, some a *sybille* (which is the French word for seer and I love it!) and it's not just someone who has visions; it's someone who *sees* and *feels* and *experiences* the truth beneath the surface, who feels the pulse of the world and is able to channel it into something transformative, needed and necessary. (While that's not a dictionary definition, it's my definition.)

Now, because I have "the sight", does it mean I'm immune to fuck-ups because I can see what's unfolding? No.

Does it mean I can see how everything is going to end? No.

Does it mean I can figure out the lotto numbers? I bloody wish.

I'm human and part of my learning here at Earth School is to experience the human-ness of it all; but what the all-seeing aspect does offer, when I get out of my own way (and that's a daily bloody practice), is a deep and clear inner-sight, wisdom, clarity and much-needed discernment, so that when I *do* take a breath, create some space and connect in at my centre, I can see *exactly* what's going on amongst the societal manipulation and coercion.

Being all-seeing involves, first and foremost, being present and feeling what the heart feels in real time – and knowing, deep in my belly and bones, if we do *see* beyond and if we do trust what it is that we see, we come into our body, come in and down, all the way to our centre.

We connect with source as source; we remember that we are infinite, mother-loving creative life force and we're then able to assess, discern and respond accordingly. Let's be clear: that's not easy to do in a world that wants us emotionally (and physically) inflamed and reactionary, as it's much easier to divide us and create separation when we don't remember our true nature.

And from that place of connection, you show up differently, because you see and you know. You trust yourself and your vision, and your knowing and your "presence" becomes your power. You can "see" what's going on, you can read between the words that are spoken and hear what's not being said. You know when you're being lied to and you know when you meet real – because you feel what you "see".

Look, uncertainty is *not* comfy. That's the point, because it's where we grow our capacity to "see". Trusting yourself as a seer is knowing that your visions – however fleeting and/or wild or nonsensical (especially then!) – are keys and codes to shaping and spelling these times. Your inner knowing is guidance, not guesswork. It will, if you let it, whisper ideas to you before they become trends. It will see connections that others will undoubtedly miss, and it will recognize what is needed/required to heal and/or inspire – and when you trust that, you act accordingly.

To trust it means giving yourself permission to act on what you see, even and especially when it feels completely out of sync with the world around you. Creation – as I'm continually finding in my own creative process – really begins when we trust *this*, because without it, our visions stay daydreams instead of the seeds of real change.

Directly after the fullness of the Moon, this used to be a phase when my inner critic was loudest (I mean, she still definitely hangs out here, but she's no longer the loudest). It's now a place where I'm able to see everything as it is. No gloss. No fancy filters.

Discernment

I rarely, if ever, speak about *all* of what I "see", because our "sight" needs discernment. Not everyone will be ready to/want to hear or receive what we see, so we have to practise discernment as to what and how we share it. Discernment is our superpower, and while I very much want us to remember our magic, I also want us to realize and recognize that not everyone deserves access to it or is ready to receive it.

This is absolutely *not* about taming, censoring or hiding; it's about being centred and anchored in your body so that you can trust yourself – your inner sight and instincts and wisdom – to witness, feel, respond and create accordingly in any situation. This also includes recognizing that discernment is not about harsh critique; it's simply a process in which you have the power to choose what's important, what stays, what evolves and what you are ready to release with loving honesty and creative power and agency.

DISCERNMENT IS DEVOTION TO YOUR CLEAREST, TRUEST CREATIVE VISION.

The Power and Benefits of the Waning Gibbous Moon

You're creating, you're expressing yourself, you're being seen; now, at the Waning Gibbous Moon, the invitation is integration. This phase allows you to absorb what you've learned, felt and experienced so far through your creative process, and to let it land in your body, bones and being as experiential felt wisdom. This deepens your self-definition, helping you see yourself more clearly as the creatrix.

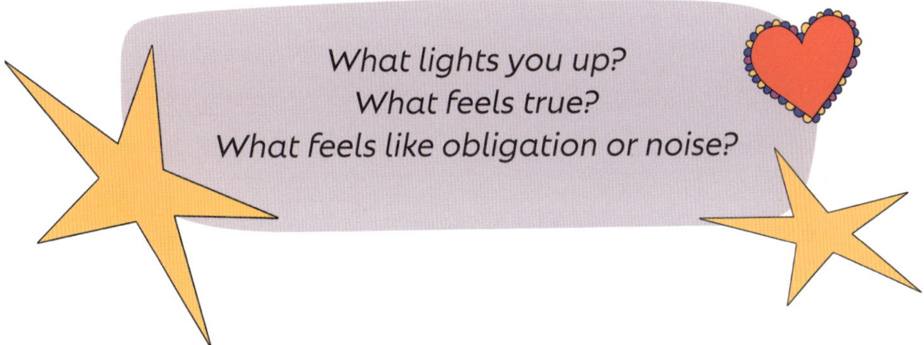

You can use this phase to define your creative identity with knowledge and power and lovingly refine it too.

With this clarity comes coherence, creating a delicious alignment between you and your projects, your energy and desires so that everything moves in a very delicious harmonic way. So use this phase to integrate it all. Define what feels true. Refine what you've learned, what you've created and what you want to carry forward. Align your energy and your intentions with clarity, and discern what is yours to hold and what it's time to release.

WANING GIBBOUS MOON MAVEN

MADAME YEVONDE

(1893–1975)

"BE ORIGINAL OR DIE."
MADAME YEVONDE

Madame Yevonde, an English photographer who pioneered the use of colour in portrait photography, is the acumination of everything significant about the Waning Gibbous Moon phase: visionary, deliberate and unapologetically original.

Best-known for her sharp yet concise motto "Be original or die", Madame Yevonde, born Yevonde Philone Cumbers in 1893, broke into the male-dominated field of photography as a young woman with no formal art training but a deep instinct for visual storytelling. She trained under Lallie Charles, a leading society photographer at the time, and very quickly broke out on her own. By 21, she'd set up her own studio, determined not to be anyone's assistant or muse but an artist in her own right.

What set her apart wasn't just that she had a camera, it was what she did with it. Yevonde was obsessed with colour at a time when most people saw it as vulgar or gimmicky. In the 1930s, she began using the Vivex colour process, which allowed for vivid, layered colour photography. It was slow, technical and unpredictable, but she saw its magic and she mastered it.

Her most famous series, the *Goddesses* project, was utterly ground-breaking. She photographed aristocratic women as mythological icons – women as Venus, Persephone, Medusa, Pandora. Drenched in colour, veiled in symbolism, dripping in drama. The series was camp, surreal and deeply feminist, because she wasn't showing women as they were expected to be, but as they chose to be seen. They were self-mythologizing masterpieces.

As well as forging new visual techniques, Yevonde was smashing cultural norms. At a time when women were expected to be subjects, not creators, she pretty much said, "Er, no thank you", and went on to carve out a space where women could be extravagant, eccentric, powerful and mythic.

Her slogan "Be original or die" was far more manifesto than marketing (although it was definitely that, too). It was both a warning shot and vow to the world: creativity is life. Sameness is death. And for women especially, originality was – and still is – a radical act, because to express yourself fully, without apology, is to reclaim power in a world that would much prefer women to be powerless. This manifesto could be seen in Yevonde's complete disinterest in following the trends of the time, for she was far more interested in creating them. She trusted her creative eye and her desire for drama and beauty and she innovated, refined and aligned her vision with her values and refused to dull her brilliance. She infused her photography with theatricality and vivid, almost dreamlike colours and made deliberate choices that turned her work into legacy.

Yevonde's art shows us that technique and rebellion *can* coexist. She was meticulous, mastering complex processes that most men couldn't even be bothered to learn. And her mind? The woman was a pure wild genius. And it's that combination – disciplined devotion, vision and defiance – that made her a woman who is still talked about and revered (although not nearly enough) today.

Yevonde reminds us that being a woman, a creatrix, isn't just about what you create; it's about how you claim the space to create it. She did it with colour, with courage, and from what I've heard, a little bit of chaos sometimes, too. She mistressed the power of composition – not just in art, but in life, and composed her images with care, arranging each element with intentionality.

So too, in this phase, do you become the creative composer of your reality. You step back, take stock and arrange your energy, your projects, your commitments into a symphony that feels deeply, unmistakably you. After the peak radiance of the Full Moon, you enter a moment of clarity. This is the time to define your originality, to refine your creations and to align your work, life and entire reality with your wild, unique truth.

The Hot Spots and Shadows of the Waning Gibbous Moon

The Full Moon is such an energetic peak that you might feel a creative dip as you move through the Waning Gibbous Moon phase. Integration needs space, so honour your energy levels and remember that the slow-down is part of the alignment process.

And while discernment is powerful, if left unchecked, it can slip into self-doubt. Be clear: are you refining from a place of creative clarity or from fear? Root your choices in trust and if, in the process, you find yourself peeking at others and wondering if you measure up (this is such a sneaky hot spot of the Waning Gibbous phase), come back to centre, your centre, and give your heart a gentle tap to remind yourself that your creative rhythm is uniquely yours. Alternatively, and I have definitely done this on a few occasions, write a Post-it note, telling yourself to "stay in your lane".

With the refining energy of this phase, there's a risk that you might fall into the realms of endless tweaking. Be aware that the edit and release process of this phase can stir up resistance, especially when you've poured energy, love, devotion and dedication into something, and that sometimes releasing and editing what is no longer necessary or required can and will make space for more magic to enter. Yet watch out for the trap of trying to perfect something that is already powerful. Sure, refine it, but don't edit away all your magic in the process.

Mistress Your Magic

Here are rituals and practices designed to help you become an energetic frequency match for your own magic and creative power during the Waning Gibbous Moon phase.

Refine the Spell Ritual

To lovingly refine your creative work/life/reality and honour your evolution with care, not critique.

You'll need

- Your current creative project (or notes/drafts)
- A candle (white or silver for clarity)
- Your journal or a piece of paper
- A pen

1. Light your candle and declare out loud:

   I refine with love. I honour my creative truth.

2. Sit with your work-in-progress. Gently review it, not with harsh eyes, but with a heart open to clarity:
   - What feels alive and true?
   - What needs a gentle edit or polish?
   - What no longer belongs and can be released?

3. Make your refinements slowly and intentionally, as if you're tending to a cherished piece of art (because you are).

4. Close by journaling a short note to your future self, honouring the progress you've made. Then extinguish your candle safely.

This is a ritual I use each and every time I start the edits of each book, because refinement from a place of devotion, not criticism, strengthens your creative work and your self-trust. It turns editing – whether it's a project, life or your reality – into an act of creative care.

The Align Your Energy Practice

To align your body, mind and creative intentions with your truest desires.

You'll need

- A quiet space
- A journal or a piece of paper
- A pen
- Simply time to reflect

1. Take three deep breaths, feeling your feet on Mumma Earth, and let your body soften to receive.
2. Place your hands on your heart and ask:
    - What am I truly working toward?
    - What do I want my creative work/life to feel like?
    - How do I want my days to feel?
3. Reflect or journal your answers.
4. From this place of clarity, write down one to three actions you can take this week to align more deeply with your creative truth.
5. Repeat this alignment check-in daily during the Waning Gibbous Moon phase. When you align your intentions with your actions, you move from scattered to focused, and from reactive to intentional. This phase is about coherence, so let your choices reflect your deepest creative desires.

The Art of Discernment Practice

To practise the sacred art of letting go and making space for what truly matters.

You'll need

- A piece of paper
- A pen
- *Optional:* a small bowl in which to burn the ripped-up paper afterwards

1. Write down what is no longer serving your creative journey – fears, old projects, doubts, comparisons, whatever is cluttering/disrupting your creative energy and power.
2. Underneath, write:

   I release what no longer aligns with my truth. I open space for more magic, more of what lights me up.

3. Tear the paper into small pieces and safely burn the scraps.
4. Close by placing your hands over your heart and saying out loud:

   I honour what has been. I trust what is to come.

WANING GIBBOUS MOON

Wisdom · Coherence · Field Transmission

The Science: Coherence and knowing create a sense of stability in the field. Once the wave has collapsed into form, your system recalibrates. Your nervous system, brain and body begin to attune to your new frequency. This is where alignment becomes embodiment – your energy is no longer *just* broadcasting; it's informing the environment around you.

The Magic: This is embodied magic. The frequency you've held is now living in your field. You've become the transmitter. Your lived experience is a message to the field and to others: "This is what's possible." This is what resonance looks and feels like when it's really lived.

The Spell: Integrate before you initiate. Let yourself feel into and fully experience what's been created. Let your body register the change. My personal rule? To only ever teach, share or speak from what has truly been lived and experienced.

The Waning Gibbous Moon phase is not a come-down from the high of the Full Moon (although it might feel a bit like that until you fully practise working with it); it's a pause after the celebration, a time where you can catch your breath, gather and integrate your wisdom, and refine your magic into something even sharper and more true-to-you. It's where you ask:

- What feels aligned?
- What deserves my energy?
- What is true for me, right now?

It's where you:

- Define your creative identity and your body of work, claiming your originality with clarity and pride.
- Refine your creations and your process, honouring the details that elevate your magic and power.
- Align your energy, your intentions and your actions with your truest desires and vision.
- Discern, with love, what no longer fits, releasing what drains your power to make space for what fuels your fire.

This phase invites you to become the creatrix of your life and work. Like Madame Yevonde arranging her worlds in vivid, defiant colour, you tend and honour each element with care. You choose your palette, your tempo, your voice, your outfit and you learn how the process of letting go is a fierce practice of refinement. It's a deeper devotion to your clearest, most authentic expression.

In this phase, you remember that you aren't here to follow someone else's map or to dilute your vision to fit the crowd; no, you're here to create and respell reality in your own colours, in your own rhythm, in your own fierce originality.

WANING QUARTER MOON

REVELATIONS. REVOLUTIONS

"TRUTH.
TRUTH.
TRUTH . . .
SO THAT YOU BECOME BOTH THE REVELATION AND THE REVOLUTION THAT YOU'RE CRAVING . . ."

At the Waning Quarter Moon, the energy levels you expressed at the Full Moon are truly over. You're much less interested in the outside world, and in turn, now have inner sight about, well, just about everything.

Waning Quarter Moon Energy and How It Affects You

The Waning Quarter Moon is a great time to practise balance, because as with the Waxing Quarter Moon, when you may feel a tendency to "rush" and "do" just because you can, in this phase, you may feel a tendency to come to a complete standstill. Lethargy and a "no-do" vibe can kick in, so while this

WANING QUARTER MOON

- Slow down.
- Seek truth (both your own and that of other people).
- Edit (life and on paper).
- Make sure that what you're left with after the harvest – the fruit of your work – will sustain and nourish and fortify.
- Trust your revelations, even if they scare you.
- Witness and respond to your inner revolution.

Sounds: Fierce and fiery. Think: Yeah Yeah Yeahs, Patti Smith, PJ Harvey.

Essential oils and herbs: Black pepper (catalyst energy), patchouli (grounding revolution).

Extra-sensory anchor: Sip a bitter herbal tea (like dandelion, mugwort or chicory). Let the bitterness awaken clarity and the sharp, sobering energy of truth in your body and being.

Moon phase is definitely a cue to slow down, don't stop entirely. This phase holds lots of opportunity to use the inner sight we activated last Moon phase to break down old ways and forms that are no longer of use to you, your creativity and how you show up in the world.

This is what I lovingly refer to as our "rebellion in service of truth" phase. The revelations come because you slow down, dare to look beneath the surface and ask yourself:

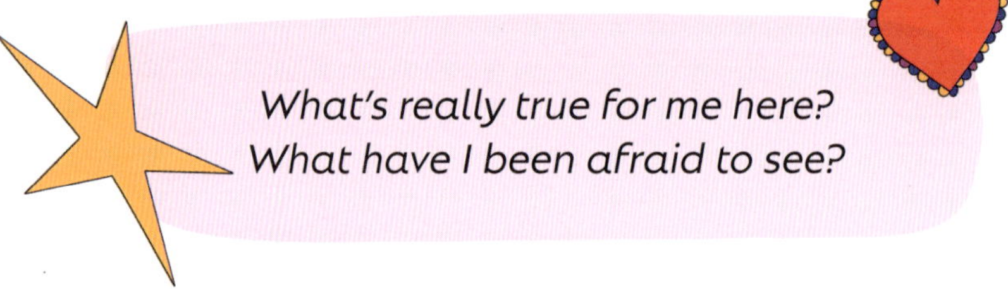

And revolutions are born from what it is that you discover here. This doesn't have to be a turn-your-whole-life-upside-down-overnight situation (although it might be); it can be the choice to stop betraying and abandoning yourself, and to stop living by rules you never agreed to.

It's in this phase that:

- You see what has held you back, and you choose to liberate yourself.
- You see where you've censored your voice, and you choose to let it roar.
- You see where you've compromised your truth, and you choose to reclaim it.

The Waning Quarter Moon: A Riff

I'm wildly passionate about journaling, because it's in those pages that I get to come undone, on my terms and in my own time. I unfold and unfurl my entire story – and it's in this phase, the Waning Quarter Moon, that journaling leads me directly to my SHE spot.

Now, your SHE spot – and we all have one – feels exquisitely vulnerable and divinely delicious. Think of the best orgasm you've ever experienced: that's the feeling we're looking to experience when we hit our SHE spot. It's total runny honey. It's when what you're creating feels so real and true and aligned with your heart, with who you truly are, and magic is present there.

Except, we oftentimes ignore it, because in order to access that vulnerable, yet *really* delicious runny honey that can be found at your SHE spot, as I'm sure you've already experienced when you've created, well . . . anything, it can be painful. It can evoke feelings that have previously been pushed down deep into the darkness and which lurk in our shadows. Then we get fearful that if we do touch our SHE spot, we'll express ourselves in a way that might make us do that snotty-nosed, ugly cry. At the very least.

Or we might discover something too bright, too powerful, that fills us up with so much light and love we might implode in on ourselves. It's where the parts of my story that I'm sure I'll be set on fire for telling reside. Where the stories of the things we did to keep ourselves alive reside. Where what we long for, our desires and hunger reside.

There's a chance you've got really used to telling the "edited" version, the acceptable, carefully rehearsed version of the story, and making art and living life in alignment with that; so accessing the SHE spot and telling/making/sharing the yet-to-be-articulated truth-art might be new to you.

It's my place of vulnerability and it feels so good to know it exists and that's why I give it space. It's the place I access to create, to write and respell my *entire reality*. When I know that I can access this spot for the gold, the runny honey, I let it flow and then – once words, marks, colours are on a page? I can start to witness what's mine, and what's for the collective.

The more we access the SHE spot, the more we trust ourselves and the less we're rocked or wobbled by what others might think and feel. The SHE spot is the place where vulnerability, truth and magic meet, because when you *know* this place, the practice of creating art, relationships, entire realities, is deliciously devotional and in direct integrity and alignment with you and what matters. *Sigh.*

To activate *your* SHE spot, which ultimately is to create art – or a life – that's in alignment with your heart and body truth, is always to move from the inside out. It means your choices, your creations, your rhythm and your relationships reflect who you really are, not who you were taught to be.

Now, this might seem like wishful thinking and I get that, because while it's possible (and I know this, because for 96 per cent of the time, it's how I'm creating and experiencing my own life), it's not without friction. It's not without grief. But it is absolutely possible and really bloody worth it.

Creating from your heart and body truth – your SHE spot – is like tuning in to a deeper current, an ancient/future feminine frequency. When you trust that frequency, even when it's terrifying, that is alignment. And it's here that you really get to practise what it feels like.

You start by listening. Not to your fear. Not to the algorithm. To the part of you that knows what makes you feel most alive. You get radically honest. You ask:

What do I really want?
What do I really believe?
Who am I when no one's watching?

And then you build and create and respell from there.

You let your "yes" be sacred, and your "no" be a complete sentence. You stop chasing external milestones and start creating internal milestones: joy, peace, resonance, expansion, truth.

You accept that alignment will cost you certain things like approval, ease and illusions, but it will return you to yourself. And while creating from your

SHE spot doesn't mean you'll never doubt yourself, it *does* mean that you'll know where to return when you do.

Come Undone

In this Moon phase, you're being invited – no, dared – to come undone. Not because you've failed or because something's broken, but because you are no longer the version of yourself that's trying to hold it all together.

This is an unthreading of old masks, coping strategies and tightly wound stories that were stitched together for your safety, not your power. It's an undoing from what is no longer yours. You unravel from the old patterns and programmes – societal and familial – so that you can re-weave, retell, respell by your own rhythm, your own truth, not the world's expectations to create something completely different (*thank fuck for that*)!

It's also a direct rebuttal to the constant and relentless pressure to stay strong, stay graceful, stay pleasing. You're not breaking *down*. You're breaking *open*. This can feel similar to The Tower tarot card. A card that can cause even the most seasoned tarot lovers to sweat a little, and I get it: no one wants to have to consider that their shit is falling all the way apart, right?!

Now, this is very "Tower" of me to say, but the fear of the Tower is often rooted in misunderstanding, which is also indicative of this part of the creative cycle: as we come into greater alignment with our personal truth, there's a chance that we will also be misunderstood, because we're no longer the version of ourselves that other people are comfortable with.

For the longest time, my life felt like a procession of what some call "dark nights of the soul", but what I lovingly refer to as "Tower moments". Moments when everything that I thought was true and real has broken/crumbled/crashed/fucked up/*All. The. Things*. I'd witnessed the crumble, I'd definitely felt the grief, and because I've worked so intimately with this in my own experience, over and over again, I *know* that I'm never there indefinitely. I also know that the *only* thing left to do when you are deep *in it* is to take a deep breath and, on the exhale, *choose* to surrender to it and to come all the way undone.

A Tower moment occurs when the things you *thought* were solid are not. And while it can mark a breakup, job loss, identity crisis and/or some other disruptive moment, that's not the whole story . . . The Tower doesn't destroy you; it destroys what's *not* authentic, *not* stable and *not* aligned: that toxic relationship, that outdated version of yourself, that job that's draining your soul. The Tower takes it down to the ground so that we don't stay trapped. It removes what's rotting beneath the surface so that real growth can occur.

If, upon seeing the Tower card or experiencing a Tower moment, it feels doom-laden and fear-filled, here's my first invitation: don't disconnect. The Tower doesn't mean doom; it means *shift*. Something's ready and waiting to be seen and cleared. Don't ask "what's falling apart?"; instead, ask yourself:

WHAT'S BEING LIBERATED HERE. WHAT'S BEING FREED UP?

Because – and I'm not trying to be a Positive Polly here – there is *always* something better on the other side, even if you can't see it yet.

So often, to survive in our society, we're told to "hold it together" and *not* fall apart. Yet anytime you let yourself come undone, it's a reminder that nothing is permanent, that death creates new growth and that you're not meant to bloom all the time. For everything, there is a season, and it's this cyclical wisdom and knowing that that always supports me and *will* support us. It's important to stop clinging tightly to the edges of our current reality and all that we perceive as keeping us "safe". Instead, we need to unravel so that we can *fully* trust and know what we don't know (because we're contrary like that) in order to reveal our capacity to dream, create, retell and respell something we have no idea about yet, but that's absolutely already coded in our body, blood and bones.

The Power and Benefits of the Waning Quarter Moon

When I speak of Wonder Woman (which I do often because I love her), I refer to her as the Full Moon phase, when it feels like we can do *all* the things, but it's here, at the Waning Quarter Moon, that we access Wonder Woman's most potent power: the lasso of truth. You feel like you've drunk a gallon of truth serum, and your bullshit-sensing meter is cranked up HIGH. All you want is truth. You're literally a truth-seeking missile here. You ask yourself:

What's really necessary?
Does it feed and nourish me?
Is it important? Is it of service?

It's also here where we meet the inner critic, and it's here that we must befriend that critic, understand their motives; otherwise, there's a chance that our inner critic will consume us.

If you thought we were done with discernment in this phase, you'd be wrong, as the need for it now cranks up a notch (or ten). That's because we have the potential to become ruthless in our pursuit of what matters. Our tongue becomes sharp, yet we're less articulate (and patient) in this phase, so we really need to flex our discernment muscle. Remember, discernment is *not* censorship; it's a personal practice of refinement. It's about asking what needs to be shared and *how* does it need to be shared, if at all?

Truth, conviction in what it is you're saying and doing, discernment in what stays, what goes, what's being released and making sure that what remains is strong and fortified – these are the superpowers of the Waning Quarter Moon.

WANING QUARTER MOON MAVEN

AMRITA SHER-GIL

(1913–1941)

"I AM AN INDIVIDUALIST. I DO NOT FOLLOW ANY SCHOOL. I DO NOT CARE FOR NORMS AND TRADITIONS . . . I REFUSE TO BE DICTATED TO OR BOUND BY ANYTHING."

AMRITA SHER-GIL

A sensuous, sharp-minded, free-spirited woman and artist, Amrita Sher-Gil has been called "one of the greatest avant-garde women artists of the early 20th century". She was a pioneer in modern Indian art and used her own art to claim space in a world that tried to confine her.

Amrita was born in 1913, a biracial, bicultural woman in colonial India. Her father was a Sikh aristocrat and scholar; her mother a Hungarian-Jewish opera singer. From the very beginning, she lived between worlds. She was fluent in multiple languages, trained in European art schools, and exposed to the Parisian avant-garde. But what made her extraordinary wasn't just her technique; it was how she synthesized everything she was into something totally original.

Her early work, created in Paris, had echoes of the post-Impressionists, but even then, there was a difference. Her gaze was introspective, her palette earthy, her subjects often brown-skinned women painted not as exotic curiosities (as was so often the case in those times), but as thinking, feeling, real people.

And then, she returned to India. And this is where everything changed.

Back home, Amrita shed the safety of European recognition and dove into the richness of her roots. She travelled through rural villages, sketched ordinary people and immersed herself in the rhythms of everyday Indian life. She stopped painting for applause and started painting from her truth. The result? A visual language that was earthy, raw, luminous and deeply feminist.

Works such as *Three Girls* (1935), *Bride's Toilet* (1937) and *The Story Teller* (1937) show Indian women as soulful, complex beings. There is quiet pain in their eyes, dignity in their stillness and longing in their posture. And in portraying them this way, Amrita gave Indian women visibility on their own terms. She painted them with empathy and truth, and not the voyeurism of the Western male gaze.

As a woman, Amrita lived boldly. Sensual, intellectually fierce, bisexual and uninterested in being obedient to society's ideas of who or what she *should* be, she smoked, wore men's clothing, engaged in passionate relationships with both women and men, and refused to apologize for any of it. She was magnetic, glamorous, witty, sharp – and she knew it. But her allure wasn't just an aesthetic. It was the power of someone deeply rooted in herself and her truth.

Amrita Sher-Gil lived and created as an undivided act of truth and self-expression.

No choosing between the personal and the political. No separating the art from the artist. Her art was a mirror that she used to reflect the world as she saw it and to honour the people, especially the women, who were so often erased from it.

She died heartbreakingly young, at 28. But in that short span, she changed Indian art forever. And she left behind both a body of work and a blueprint for how to live as a female artist: with honesty, passion and a refusal to ever, ever dilute your truth.

The Hot Spots and Shadows of the Waning Quarter Moon

This phase can and will stir deep emotional currents. You might feel grief for what's ending, frustration at what's not working, or excitement (mixed with fear) for what's to come. Give yourself space to feel it all. Because revelations? They're not always gentle. Seeing and experiencing your truth can be confronting. You may realize you've outgrown parts of your work, your life, even your creative identity. Let discomfort always be the spark, never the stop sign.

Now, even when you *know* change is needed, it can feel hard to let go of familiar patterns or projects. Fear of the unknown might – most likely will – creep in. Remember: revolution always involves risk, but also there is always a reward, I promise! What I will say is that revelations and revolutions *do* demand energy, so honour your body and your nervous system in this phase, and beware of swinging from intensity fatigue (it's a thing!) to, well, chaos. Discernment is still your ally here. Release what needs to go, but keep tending to what still holds true value – we definitely want to burn away what's false, but not every moment has to be a Tower moment, right?

MEET AND BEFRIEND YOUR INNER CRITIC

I want to take a moment now to invite you to face and meet your critic, because if you don't, it will show up each and every cycle and potentially try to undermine you . . . Ultimately, it wants to keep you safe and stop you from failing and fucking up, but we know that this is how we grow, so begin by listing some of the things your critic tells you about who you are. Don't question whether they're right or wrong; just think about that moment when you want to create: what do you hear?

List them all. It may be you've been told these things by others – the critic stores it all to use against you – so anything that feels slightly negative and, more importantly, stops you creating, stops you showing up in the world in your true awesome colours. Write it all down, because you can guarantee your critic knows *all* about it.

As you write them out, experience what those words make you feel about yourself – do you feel angry, do you feel small? (I know this might not feel altogether pleasant, but we *do* need to go there.)

Does the way your critic speaks replicate your mumma? Or maybe your dad? Or a teacher? Y'see, the critic is something of a shape-shifter, and isn't above morphing into the shape and voice of someone who has told us we're not good enough in our past.

Can you get an image of your critic? Maybe you know who the voice belongs to? Is there a colour or a shape that you feel represents your critic?

Set yourself a time limit and *really* get to know your critic. I encourage you to set time limits because it creates a container for you to explore these not-so-comfy places. Half an hour should be plenty, and when you're done, give yourself a big cuddle and play Taylor Swift's "Shake It Off" REALLY LOUD.

The good news is, when you get to know your critic a little more intimately, it can be a powerful friend. You are in a lifetime relationship with each other and learning about it is a forever job. The good news is, there are three things that your inner critic is doing to actually help you:

1. Your enemies grow you, so by facing your critic, the stronger you can now become.
2. Your critic knows no boundaries – everything is fair game for comment and nothing is out of bounds as far as your critic is concerned. Your critic knows all of your weak points and will fire directly at them with pinpoint precision. Your critic will go there. But in facing your critic, you can clearly see your areas and times of vulnerability and develop super-strong boundaries about what's acceptable and what's not to continually fortify yourself.
3. It operates in generalities and definitely isn't one for detail. For example, it might say "you're an idiot" but won't tell you what it means by that. It tells you what you should or shouldn't do, but doesn't really appreciate what it takes for you to do those things. This gives us a major opportunity to question the validity of the critic's statement, which means we get to take back control. Hurrah!

Understanding the inner critic's role in helping you to build your inner authority and boundaries within your creative and respelling process will help you to appreciate, meet and work with it a whole lot more skilfully. Just so you know, doing this work is BIG. I am loving you and *all* your parts as you explore this.

Mistress Your Magic

Here are rituals and practices to help you become an energetic frequency match for your creative power during the Waning Quarter Moon phase.

The Discomfort Draft

To turn emotional or creative discomfort into raw material for art, this practice invites you to mine the "uncomfortable" for gold.

You'll need

- A timer
- Your creative tools (journal, laptop, art supplies)
- A grounding object (such as a crystal, talisman or essential oil of your choice)

1. Set the timer for 13 minutes.
2. Write/create/riff on these heart prompts:
   - What I don't want to admit is . . .
   - The most uncomfortable truth is . . .
3. Let it be messy. Let it surprise you. No editing.
4. When the timer sounds, place your grounding object over your heart or in your palm. Breathe into your body.
5. Ask:

   Is there a creative thread in here?

6. Highlight or circle anything that wants to be explored further.

Excavation Hour: The Deep Dig

To support yourself while unearthing the raw, uncomfortable truths that lie beneath the surface – truths that need compassion, not criticism, as they come up. This is about staying present as you uncover what's been buried.

You'll need

- A timer
- A cosy blanket or shawl
- A journal or a piece of paper
- A pen
- A warm drink (herbal tea or cacao)
- Optional: headphones and a grounding playlist

1. Wrap yourself in the blanket and get comfortable: you're going in, so your body needs to feel safe.
2. Sip your warm drink slowly and consciously. Let your nervous system settle.
3. Set a timer for 22 minutes. Open your journal and riff on either of the following heart-prompts:
   - What truth have I been circling but not naming?
   - What have I buried that is now ready to be seen?
4. Free-write. Don't analyse, just let it spill onto the page. If emotions rise, pause and place your hand on your chest or your belly. Breathe. Then keep writing.
5. When the timer ends, close your journal and place it under your pillow or near your bed.
6. Let your subconscious continue working overnight.

Truth Activation Ritual

To take the truth you've discovered and begin shaping it into something shareable, useful or revolutionary – whether that's art, action or aligned decision-making.

You'll need

- A candle (any colour)
- Three index cards or small pieces of paper
- A marker or pen
- A fireproof bowl or jar
- Your journal

1. Light the candle and say:

   I am ready to work with what I now know.

2. Write three truths you've uncovered recently – one per card. These can be painful, powerful or wildly inconvenient. Be honest.
3. Flip over each card and write a way you could activate this truth. A boundary. A creative act. A change.
4. Choose one card to burn (or tear up). As it burns, say:

   This truth fuels my freedom.

5. Paste or tape the other two into your journal. They are your creative seeds.
6. Close with this heart-riff prompt:

   If I honoured this truth fully, what might I create next?

7. Blow out the candle to seal the ritual.
8. The Waning Quarter Moon marks a turning point: truth has been revealed, and we're called to clear space for what must go. This ritual transforms revelation into revolution by helping you make peace and choose what to carry into your next creative cycle. It honours the alchemy of endings and emotional wisdom.

WANING QUARTER MOON

Release · Truth · Recalibration

The Science: In quantum terms, when you stop observing, the wave returns to potential, so when you release your focus, it dismantles the structure. You disrupt the momentum of a pattern by no longer feeding it with your attention, awareness and emotion.

The Magic: This is the magic of conscious undoing. Removing your energy from what no longer serves and letting the pattern unravel. The next timeline cannot fully emerge while you're still clinging to the last.

The Respell: Cut the cords and collapse loops. Withdraw your gaze and call back and reclaim your power from the old reality. You are creating What Comes Next. Let this be a mother-loving, really bloody liberating total disintegration.

The Waning Quarter Moon is the rebellious reveal-er. It shows you what no longer fits, what can no longer be denied, and what is begging for retelling and respelling:

What is true?
What no longer fits?
What stories am I finally done apologizing for?

This phase will make you want to revolt against narratives that aren't yours, against habits that keep you small, and against the invisible rules that were never meant to contain your wildness. There's no censoring, no shrinking and no sanitizing. There's the burn and release of what needs to go, there's the inevitable grief for what no longer fits and there's the need to stop feeling like you must hold it all together. Now's the time to come undone so that you can reclaim your creative agency and power. Your voice. Your authority over the shape and rhythm of your life, your art, your expression and your reality.

This is a sacred part of the cycle: it's the editor's red pen, the boundary line, the sacred "no" that makes space for a deeper "yes". It's here that your vision (sight) and the bigger vision, become sharper – what was once vague now becomes precise. You cut away the excess, letting the core message, your truth, stand strong. You clarify your purpose, not just in terms of what you're creating but why, as you prepare to descend back into the void of possibility, the cosmic womb, carving out the space for what will come next not by slowing down passively, but by actively clearing the path.

The Waning Quarter Moon teaches you that your revelations are road signs. Your revolutions are rites and that your creative power expands every time you choose yourself. Again. And again. And again.

WANING CRESCENT MOON

REFLECT. RESPECT. CELEBRATE.

REST NOW.
YOU'VE COME A LONG WAY.
LOOK AT HOW FAR YOU'VE COME.
WHAT YOU'VE ACHIEVED.
WHAT YOU'VE LEARNED.
WHO YOU *ARE*.
YOU EBB AND YOU FLOW. YOU RISE AND YOU FALL.
YOU'RE RHYTHMIC.
YOU'RE CYCLIC.
YOU'RE BLOODY INCREDIBLE . . .

The Waning Crescent Moon is the final visible sliver of the Moon's 28-day (or so) journey around the Earth. After being full and bright, the Moon has gradually been growing dimmer and becoming less visible and, eventually, the light disappears completely, which is the final stage before the New Moon phase, when the cycle begins all over again.

So, you know when you've had a *really* long day and you've had a bath and you get into your bed and you just feel your body sink and surrender to the mattress below it? You take a breath, and you're thankful to have the bath and the bed and you take another big deep breath and you surrender some more? That's *this* Moon phase.

WANING CRESCENT MOON

- Rest.
- Crystalize.
- Distil.
- Reflect.
- Journal a list of your cycle's highlights and lessons.

Playlist: Soulful, slow, intimate. Think: Joni Mitchell, Norah Jones, Tracy Chapman.

Essential oils and herbs: Myrrh (deep reflection), sandalwood (spiritual connection).

Extra-sensory anchor: Journal in bed, wear something that feels like a hug. Honour your cycle. Honour yourself.

Waning Crescent Moon Energy and How It Affects You

It's a time to rest and reflect. To drop deep into dreamtime, in both your sleeping and your awake hours, allowing your big and beautiful brain to have a clear-out and for you to start receiving intel *all over again*.

There's a good chance that nothing is making sense here, because as the Moon herself is waning to "no"-thing, so too is this cycle. It's reaching its end. So, it's here that you can feel between worlds: you may feel like you're completing one cycle or dreaming into the next and that you don't know what's real and what's not. It's like the season of Samhain, the pagan/Celtic festival that's celebrated at the end of October, also known as Witches' New Year, when the veil between worlds is at its thinnest. If you're someone who experiences a menstrual cycle, it's like the void space between not bleeding and bleeding. That point where you've cried and you're in the dreamiest nonlinear space; you get clumsy and can't remember why you've put your phone in the fridge (please say it's not just me?!).

This phase is an invitation to reflect on everything that's unfolded within the cycle that's passed – the rise, the descent and the mysteries in-between – and to turn inward and gather the wisdom of the journey. To witness the steps you've taken, the courage you've cultivated and the spells you've cast.

Respect your process. The energy it took for you to bring your visions to life, the seasons of your creativity – the wild bursts of inspiration, the time spent in disciplined devotion to your art and creation and the digging and excavating, the self-discoveries you've made. Honour the woman you've been and are in every phase of the cycle. Give her a wink, blow her a kiss and give her the biggest hug – you deserve your deepest reverence.

Celebrate it all. The victories and the lessons, all that you've created and shared (and not shared), and the ones that are still simmering beneath the surface waiting to be dreamed into being. This is where you raise a toast – with green juice, tea or gin – to yourself and your creative courage.

The Waning Crescent Moon: A Riff

The liminality of this phase means that your instincts and intuition are at their highest. It's where we're most open to receive, so trust what comes through for you. It's a creative pit-stop, a chance to refill and refuel, and to trust that

I DON'T NEED TO FORCE THE NEXT WAVE OF CREATIVITY. BECAUSE I KNOW THAT IT'S COMING. IT ALWAYS DOES.

This cyclical wisdom gives our nervous system permission to rest and recharge.

For many reasons that I've spent far too many hours therapizing, I have always given rest a strong side-eye. I believed that rest equated laziness, that it was a weakness. And I know from working with thousands of women who are sensitive, brilliant, intuitive and creative, that rest can also feel like losing relevance and/or momentum, or that rest is for someone else: women without children, without deadlines, without pressure, basically *not* them. Never them. And that's because we've all been sold a straight-line story.

What if rest isn't the reward that you earn once everything's done? What if rest is the resource that lets you keep going?

Because, and I hate to break it to you, the to-do list will *never* be done. The inbox will never be empty. The world will always be asking for more. And if we wait until it's all handled to rest, we never will.

But the Moon? She reflects a different story. Her cycle is proof that we get to go round again, and it's in this final phase – the Waning Crescent, the balsamic Moon, the darkening Moon – that she reminds us that we don't lose our magic when we rest: we recharge it and we receive more.

We've been conditioned to give until we're empty, we're praised for self-sacrifice; so to choose to receive can feel indulgent, lazy and sometimes terrifying, especially if we've been taught that needing anything makes us less than and not worthy of more. That's why when life, love, abundance and/or ease offers itself up to us, many of us freeze, flinch even, because receiving would mean that we matter (you do, BTW), that we're worthy (you are, BTW) and that we *can* be loved, celebrated and supported without transaction.

Because to receive is to be open to intimacy, pleasure and support (and to magic and creative power and wild dreams and visions).

When the world has not been safe for you to receive – in this lifetime, past lifetimes – it can feel risky, but I want to share that *despite* what you've been told or believe, you DO deserve to be full, fed, sourced and lit up. And when you're open to receive, you don't block the flow, you expand it and you become a walking, talking and (in my case) leopard-print and red-lipstick-wearing example that joy, support and rest aren't scarce, that

WHEN A WOMAN LEARNS TO RECEIVE, SHE'S NOT BEING SELFISH. SHE'S REWIRING HISTORY, BREAKING GENERATIONAL CURSES AND RESPELLING REALITY.

This phase has become my monthly space to rest without shame (and that's still a practice BTW), knowing that each time I choose to rest here, even if it's for an hour, I'm returning, self-sourcing, to regather, reweave, re-vision.

Now, not doing, not creating, not writing and not being in action is scary and can often feel like we're not "progressing", but we can't skip rest.

I mean you can, but as I mentioned earlier, you *will* break, exhaust yourself and burn out – and of that I have no doubt and all the proof.

That's why we work with our cycles and rhythmic intelligence, so that with each cycle, we can die to what has gone before, pulling away from our "responsibilities", and we can reside in the darkness of the not-knowing. It's in not knowing that we receive our visions and renew our powers, so that we're revitalized and rejuvenated.

Seeing in the Dark

When we're in the dark of the Moon, we're in the liminal, the in-between, the fertile blackness, and it's here that if we stop producing, pleasing and performing we can *really* access our magic and creative power, because the dark – both literal and symbolic – is where we come back to ourselves.

So *of course* we've been taught to fear the dark. To fear stillness. To fear solitude. To associate the unknown with danger rather than initiation.

Darkness removes the noise, the light and the distractions we use to keep ourselves numb or busy, and encourages us to sit with what we've buried, denied or avoided and with what we're yet to dream and vision and what it is we know and can see. It's *all available* here, and I won't lie, that can feel excruciating, but also extremely exquisite. Because it's real.

Take a deep breath, close your eyes and be in the darkness of the unknown. The dark has always been women's territory. It's where the magic brews in the cosmic cauldron – the void, the place of *no*-thing and *total* possibility.

Let it remind you that the unknown *is* known to us. It's the fertile ground for *all* creative possibility. We *do* know what to do here.

Whenever the Moon goes void-of-course in astrological terms, we're in unknown territory until it moves into its next astrological sign. It's similar when day turns to night. When being awake turns to deep sleep. When the season moves from autumn into winter.

When the Moon goes dark, just as it does every cycle before it becomes new, it's no longer visible in the sky and we're left without its light, plunged into darkness and forced to be in the dark, in the unknown.

But we're not afraid of the dark, remember? It's where we grow strong. It's where, if we let ourselves, we're able to rest, repair and regenerate. To tune out all the external information and noise and, instead, turn inward and tune in to our own magic and wisdom to receive our deepest visions and insight.

The Power and Benefits of the Waning Crescent Moon

This phase offers you the space to let everything you've learned, created and become land. To rest and digest is the quiet magic – it turns experience into wisdom, action into understanding – and it's here that your creative growth and realizations settle into your bones.

It's your invitation to fill up your well, because that's a necessity *and* out of devotion to your future self. I don't want to sound like an overused meme, but rest (and by that, I mean restorative rest) *is* an act of creative rebellion in a culture that worships production and output. It gives you a chance to reflect on the cycle that you've just experienced and sharpens your self-awareness and self-knowing. You get to see, feel and witness what worked, what felt good, what drained you and what lit you up. This clarity will guide you into your next creative chapter with more ease and alignment.

Finally, we don't talk about or partake in celebration and reverence *nearly* enough. When you take time to celebrate yourself and your creative journey, you amplify your magnetism and creative momentum for the next cycle.

WANING CRESCENT MOON MAVEN

FAITH RINGGOLD

(1930–2024)

"I THINK OF MY ART AS MY VOICE. IT'S WHAT I HAVE TO SAY ABOUT THE WORLD I LIVE IN, AND IT'S ABOUT WHO I AM AND HOW I WOULD LIKE THINGS TO BE."

FAITH RINGGOLD

American artist and author Faith Ringgold is a luminous example of how a woman can honour herself, her work, and her lineage with clarity and creativity.

Born in Harlem in 1930, Ringgold's life and art were deeply rooted in the rich cultural tapestry of her community. Her mother, a fashion designer and seamstress, nurtured her early artistic inclinations.

In the 1960s, Faith began creating politically charged paintings, such as the *American People* series. Later, she pioneered the art of the story quilt, blending painting, fabric and narrative to tell stories that centred on Black women's experiences. Her 1983 quilt *Who's Afraid of Aunt Jemima?* reimagined the stereotypical figure as an African American businesswoman, challenging prevailing narratives and celebrating Black female empowerment.

Her use of fabric wasn't accidental. She turned sewing and weaving, often dismissed as "craft" or "women's work", into fine art. She once said that she didn't see people who looked like her in the art that she studied, and that if Black women weren't visible in museums or history books, then she'd weave them into existence. Stitch by stitch, she weaved a new societal fabric with the faces of her people, and she made them vivid, joyful, angry and radiant.

As a Black woman artist in the 1960s and '70s, she was told that her work wasn't "real" art, but she believed that her lived experience deserved to be seen and remembered. Her quilts were documents of stories not told. Of inner worlds. Of outer struggles. Of Black joy, family, politics, resistance.

Faith lived through segregation, racism and sexism, and didn't look away; she preserved her reality, so that her granddaughters would have a visual inheritance of pride, power and possibility. She honoured herself by refusing to erase herself; she celebrated herself by centring herself with ancestral responsibility; and she passed on that torch with fierce love.

She fought against exclusion, protested at museums, challenged racism and sexism, and refused invisibility *by* creating. She wrote children's books. She taught. She mentored. She lifted up other women *with* her, to weave their stories into her quilts, to make her personal life part of her art.

Faith Ringgold shows us that you must not wait for the world to validate your vision. Her life and work illuminate a path for ALL women to honour themselves, their work, and their lineage with courage, creativity, and conviction, and to encourage others to do the same.

The Hot Spots and Shadows of the Waning Crescent Moon

After a full cycle of creation, you may fear the quiet, wondering if the spark will ever return. I speak from experience when I say, yes, it does and it will. Always. Trust the cycle and trust yourself. Your creativity hasn't gone anywhere: like you, it's resting and recharging. Creative emptiness is *the* most fertile space for What Comes Next.

I also get the fear that if we stop, we'll never gain creative momentum again. But it's the opposite. When we rest, we re-energize and replenish. Be mindful of slipping into self-critique, regret, or harsh judgement; instead, witness yourself and your experience with compassion and love.

The biggest hot spot (and this is a personal one for me) is that it's tempting to skip the celebration of what you have achieved so far and rush directly into the next thing. But celebration seals your creative spells with joy and magnetizes more of the same. Let yourself feel the good feels – *please*!

Mistress Your Magic

Here are rituals and practices designed to help you become an energetic frequency match during the Waning Crescent Moon phase.

Rest as Ritual Practice

To choose rest as an act of creative power and devotion to your rhythm.

You'll need

- A cosy space in which to rest (such as your bed, bath or a sacred corner that you create)
- Optional: an "all is calm" playlist, blanket, herbal tea and/or favourite scents

1. Set up your rest space with intention and devotion.
2. Before you settle down in it, place one hand on your belly and one hand on your heart and say:

   Rest restores my magic.
   Rest honours my rhythm.

3. Now rest deeply – nap, daydream, soak in a bath. Release the urge to do and simply let yourself be.
4. Rest is where your creative soil becomes fertile again. Choosing rest turns pause into power.

The Cycle of Me Ritual

To honour and integrate the journey in this cycle and witness your growth with reverence.

You'll need

- A journal or a notebook
- A pen
- Candle (white or gold for reflection and illumination)

1. Light your candle and take a few breaths (the deeper and noisier the exhale the better!), as you reflect on the cycle you've just experienced.
2. In your journal, start a list titled: "Who I Became This Cycle". Then write freely. Celebrate every step, every lesson, every moment of bravery and beauty.
3. Next, write: "What I Honour About Myself As a Creatrix This Cycle". Pour gratitude onto the page. Name your resilience, your devotion, your wild courage – give it all air time.
4. Close your eyes and place your hands on your heart. Say out loud:

   I am a creatrix and I honour my cyclical wisdom and the reality I create.

5. Blow out the candle to seal the ritual, or let it burn safely as you rest.
6. Reflection gives you clarity, respect deepens your devotion, and witnessing your growth allows you to enter the next cycle empowered and whole.

A Celebration Practice

To honour your creative journey with celebration and joy.

You'll need

- Small objects that represent your creative wins (notes, photos, tokens)
- A surface to lay them out (think of it as an altar to your creative cycle)
- Creative supplies, such as paper, colouring pens, glue

1. Arrange your objects in a circle, symbolizing the completion of your creative cycle.
2. Now, place a hand on your heart and bow to your own creativity – you're incredible.
3. As you look at your circle, no matter how big or small, stand or sit and say out loud:

   I celebrate my creations.
   I celebrate my creative power.

4. *Optional:* close your celebration by dancing to your favourite song. The lunar cycle that is ending may have had a standout tune that you listened to while you were creating, or there may be a song that feels super-poignant – music and movement are my favourite way to seal any spell!
5. This celebration closes the cycle with joy and gratitude, anchoring your creative power and preparing you to enter the next phase with an open, abundant heart.

At every Dark Moon, I like to make page art in my journal that celebrates the cycle that's just been. I'll add words and images that celebrate the past cycle, so I have a visual celebration of each win and/or lesson. If I have a note from someone who commissioned a piece of art and loved it, I'll add that.

Now is the big, deep and audible exhale moment of the cycle – *ahhhhh*.

It's an opportunity to reflect on the cycle that you've experienced as a living, breathing creation and to digest all that you've learned along the way. Witness who you've become (including the grief and rage you let go – those old thoughts, beliefs, stories or unhelpful identities). Look at what you've created with your hands and heart, and how each phase of the Moon has been a mirror reflecting your own respelling of your reality.

To manifest, rewrite and respell reality, you must relax and receive, and it's our rhythmic intelligence that teaches the nervous system it's safe to do so. Your nervous system learns and, more importantly, remembers through rhythm – repetition, familiarity, breath and the pulse of each phase felt through the body, somatically. A woman who listens to her body, honours her cycle in each and every phase, and trusts her rhythmic intelligence, becomes a woman who doesn't need external validation to trust her vision.

That trust is built when you honour and respect the energy that you've invested, the courage you've summoned and the devotion you've sustained, and show deep reverence for the cycle itself – the phases of ideation, expansion, rebellion and rest, and how they all support the wholeness. FYI, "whole" is the only "goal" when you're rhythmically and rebelliously creating.

Celebrate that you *chose* to create, to show up, to breathe life into your visions, to turn your life and reality into living art. You and your story, your creations and your life, your creative power,and your magic deserve reverence.

This is *not* the end of your journey. This is the completion of one cycle, and the beginning of the next. You are not the same woman who stood at the threshold of the last New Moon. You are a woman in process (and progress) who is creating, witnessing, stirring, shaping and respelling your own reality.

You are living proof that magic is not something outside of you.

YOU ARE THE MAGIC.
YOU ARE THE SPELL.

WANING CRESCENT MOON

Rest · Surrender · Receptivity

The Science: In quantum mechanics, potential is most fluid when the system is least active. In this liminal space – where your body is still and your thought is quiet – the field becomes more responsive to subtle, emotional signals and we return to imagination, dream and frequency as the architects of form.

The Magic: This is dream-space magic. You're celebrating what's been seeded and created as you return to the in-between, the place where logic dims and inner knowing emerges once again. You *become* the field. This is the deepest creative feminine state.

The Respell: Slow down, soften your focus and let go of the need to shape and do. Allow yourself to be dreamed by the version of reality that is already seeking you.

PART THREE

RESPELL YOUR REALITY FOR LIFE

CREATE YOUR OWN RESPELL REALITY MAP

THE LUNAR CYCLE IS A FEMININE MAP THAT INVITES YOU TO GET CURIOUS ABOUT AND FASCINATED BY YOUR OWN EMOTIONAL AND FELT EXPERIENCE AS A CREATRIX, SO CONSIDER THIS YOUR INVITATION TO MAP YOUR OWN CREATIVE CYCLE, ALIGNED WITH THE PHASES OF THE MOON AND WOVEN WITH YOUR DESIRES, YOUR RITUALS AND *YOUR* SEASONS.

Your Respell Reality Map

Claim Your Intention for the Cycle

At the New Moon, ask yourself:

WHAT DO I WANT TO CREATE. CALL IN. OR BECOME IN THIS NEXT CYCLE?

Write it boldly at the top of your map and let it be your North Star.

Name Each Phase in Your Own Words

Take each Moon phase and, in your own language, claim the energy you want it to hold for you. For example:

- New Moon: seed my next chapter.
- Waxing Quarter: build momentum, step by step.
- Full Moon: share my magic.
- Waning Crescent: rest and reflect.

Be as wild, poetic or practical as you like; the idea is that you're making each phase yours.

Design Your Rituals and Anchors

For each phase, choose:

- A feeling you want to evoke and embody (e.g. brave, playful, grounded).
- A simple ritual or action to anchor you into that feeling (e.g., journaling, movement, lighting a candle, a specific creative practice).
- A song.
- A herb to burn as incense or a scent to wear as anointing oil.

For example, for the Waxing Gibbous Moon, I might write:

- *Feeling:* Fierce.
- *Ritual:* 30 minutes dedicated devotion to my creative work.
- *Song:* "Girl on Fire" by Alicia Keys.
- *Scent:* Rosemary (I personally like to mix rosemary oil with a carrier oil and apply it to my wrists and dab it on the area of the third eye, in the middle of the forehead, for clarity and alignment)

Draw or Craft Your Map

Make this visual and personal – something you'll want to return to throughout the 28-day (or so) cycle. You can make it cyclical like the Moon, in the shape of a spiral, or even quilt-inspired (with a nod to Faith Ringgold!). This is your creative compass for *your* creative cycle.

Keep It Close

Pin it above your workspace. Tuck it inside your journal. Keep it somewhere visible. Check in with it as you move through the phases. Adjust, add, celebrate. This is a map that wants to grow with you.

When you personalize your cycle, you own your power to create and respell a rhythmic reality. You become the spell-caster, the creatrix and the architect of your own experience. You stop following someone else's timeline and start living in devotion to your own.

YOUR RHYTHMIC (AND REBELLIOUS) REALITY RESPELL

IF YOU WERE HOPING FOR A ONE-SHOT TRANSFORMATION SITUATION AND YOU'VE REACHED THIS POINT, YOU'RE NOW AWARE THAT THIS IS NOT IT. THE OVER-CULTURE IS SHAPED AND FORMED BY LINEAR LOGIC, PRODUCTIVITY OBSESSION AND HYPER-MASCULINE CREATION MODELS – AND I HAVE NO INTEREST IN PERPETUATING THE SYSTEMS AND STRUCTURES THAT HAVE KEPT US BURNED OUT AND DISCONNECTED FROM OUR CREATIVE POWER AND MAGIC, THANK YOU VERY MUCH!

What I've created, curated and shared honours the feminine frequencies of creation, aligns with the lunar phases, and draws from quantum and cyclical intelligence – without requiring more deep dives and intense shadow excavation, because I'm pretty sure if you are here, you've already done a *lot* of heavy lifting where healing and shadow work is concerned.

Instead, we feel and fold time to create flow through resonance, rhythm and ritual, and to remember and reclaim *these* feminine truths:

- You are a creatrix.
- You are attuned to a cyclical, responsive universe.
- You don't need to fix yourself to create the life, art or love you desire; you remember your magic (and that you are magic) and align yourself.

You don't need to be fully healed to begin and you don't need to wait until you're "ready". The energy that creates your life responds to the frequency you hold, the rhythms you embody, and the choices you make now. Healing is cyclical, not linear. Life doesn't begin when the pain is gone; life is already happening and your magic is already (and always) available.

Each Moon phase is a portal to:

- Release stagnant emotion.
- Discharge old programming.
- Call in new stories.
- Embody ancient/future timelines.
- Align with a specific energetic shift and power-up for your creative power.

Each Moon cycle then aligns you and keeps aligning (and realigning) you to what's real and true to you – your dreams, desires and declarations – like a metronome through rhythm, repetition and ritual (and scent, sound and structure); and you respell and shape-shift reality as you attune and refine and become a compatible match for each other.

YOU RESPELL REALITY BY RHYTHMICALLY TUNING YOURSELF IN TO POSSIBILITY AND EMBODYING THE VERSION OF YOU WHO ALREADY LIVES IT.

Momentary Magic versus Sustainable Transformation

Respell Your Reality isn't just about clicking your fingers and casting a new spell and creating a new reality right away – though sometimes, yes, the shift can be instant. But the real question is: could you hold it? Could your body hold the frequency of what you've called in? Could your nervous system stay open when the manifestation arrives? Could your energy stay coherent long enough for the quantum to land?

Outdated scripts – parental voices, patriarchal conditioning, cultural pressure, internalized fears – have been encoded into our nervous systems like viral software, so it's no wonder we sabotage the things we want: the body simply can't hold what it doesn't trust and hasn't prepared for. You don't overcome these patterns with "productivity hacks" or "better time-blocking". You shift them through deliberate and embodied rhythmic intelligence.

When we live and create in sync with the Moon and our own inner tides, we can conjure change and we can contain it.

When we honour our cycles and rhythmic intelligence, we stop trying to change and fix ourselves. Yes, we may prune and edit, but we do that so more *life* becomes available – so that our capacity for *more* becomes stretchy and our bodies remember how to stay present in pleasure, in power and in expansion. That's when the quantum (and what I call the magic bit!) becomes truly accessible. It's no longer a dopamine high that we're chasing; it becomes a state that we can really sustain.

Our reality responds to frequency – the emotional, energetic and somatic tone that we carry in our body – and frequency follows rhythm. So, through following the rhythm (and ritual) of the Moon phases, we return to resonance. We signal to the nervous system: it's safe to slow down. It's safe to feel. It's safe to choose differently. This recalibrates us and brings us back to our own rhythm and our own beneath-the-surface truth. We bypass the overthinking mind and connect to the body and ancient future wisdom of our deepest knowing. It creates coherence – where your mind, body and energy align; and that's when your frequency shifts and you become the woman whose capacity is stretchy enough to hold her dreams and desires manifested.

You change your frequency by honouring your own rhythm – again and again – until reality rearranges itself to meet your truth.

Write Yourself In

Self-creation – the conscious, creative act (and art) of choosing yourself and creating in alignment with your desire, your truth and your vision from where you are right now – is what I call in my successful 28-day programme "writing yourself in".

To write yourself in is to take back the pen from the systems, stories and shadows that have written us out. It's to interrupt the dominant narrative – the one that's told us that we're too much, not enough, too loud, too soft, too late – and it's to say, "Actually, yoo-hoo – I'm here. I exist. I'm claiming space and I'm doing in on my own terms, in my own time and in my own way!"

It's a refusal to be erased.

A refusal to be reduced.

A refusal to simply be the "side piece" in your own life.

When we write ourselves in, we become visible. We're truth-full and that truth has a frequency. It vibrates. It ripples. It reshapes and respells realities.

Writing yourself in is all about presence. It's how you dress. How you say your name. How you make art, create boundaries, devote time and love to your desires; it's how you honour your body's need for rest.

Most people try to change their reality by changing their circumstances; they read all the self-help and habit-changing books, try all the supplements, even move to a different locale (I've done all of those things!). But your external experience is always downstream of your identity.

Writing yourself in – self-creation – begins by asking these three questions:

- Who am I no longer interested in being?
- Who do I choose to become?
- What stories, beliefs and energetic set-points need respelling?

This is deeper than simply "changing your mindset" to manifest a different outcome (which, as I've said previously, can work but is rarely sustainable). When you ask, and respond to, these questions and use each Moon phase to co-create, you're rewriting your own creatrix coding at the root level.

Writing yourself in is *the* most rebellious reality respell – especially if you've spent your life conforming – because you're not inventing something new, you're remembering who you were. When you write yourself in, you:

- no longer wait for permission
- stop waiting to heal fully before you begin
- no longer audition to belong

You trust your rhythmic intelligence and co-create with it to become the main character, narrator and creatrix of the most glorious adventure.

Your Future Self – Who Is She?

In the realms of self-creation, the phrase *future self* can feel . . . off. Like she's elsewhere. Like you're *chasing her* rather than *remembering her*.

In the quantum field, your future self already exists in a parallel and possible timeline. She's the version of you who has created, healed, launched, spoken, written and embodied all that you dream of and desire now. She's not a stranger, she *is* you – you're entangled: every tug of longing, creative urge or desire for more is her calling you forward.

So the good news is you're never "manifesting" from scratch. You're tuning in to the frequency of yourself that already exists. Each Moon phase becomes a way to align with her, to create in concordance with her, because when we work with the Moon, we work with our rhythmic and cyclical sense of time, and this supports us to align with our "future self", so that we bend time, we weave with it, we conjure and create with it. No hustle. *All* resonance.

The lunar cycle invites a circular, spiralling sense of time – one that returns, deepens, softens and expands – and each phase within the Moon cycle becomes a place where memory, potential and magic meet. When we chart and align our creative energy with the Moon, we understand and recognize our body as a timekeeper that's never behind and is always in tempo with life.

Here's the respell: when you choose to believe that a version of you who's already [insert your chosen dreams and desires here] already exists and you start behaving, creating, feeling from her energy, then time reshapes itself.

When you feel her in your bones and let your actions mirror hers, you collapse the timeline that existed between you. She's no longer waiting in the distance; she's folding herself into your now.

Creative women (and this has definitely been my story, too) have been taught that we have to "earn it" – whatever "it" looks and feels like for us, such as success, a career, a home, a relationship – and that it should be a "struggle".

Yet each lunar phase is a tuning fork, an invitation to choose the vibration of what it is you dream and desire, to come into alignment with it and live harmonically with it, till you become a frequency match for the version of you who already exists and so you attune, phase by phase:

- The New Moon says: dream and seed her.
- The Waxing Moon says: move like her, dress like her.
- The Full Moon says: see her and feel her.
- The Waning Moon says: shed what's not her.

Every day, in each phase and cycle, heart-riff on the following in your journal:

- What does she feel like?
- What choices would she make?
- What would shift in me today, if I truly believed I already am her?

This might sound like "basic witch" territory, but this is how I've woven lunar rhythm with quantum resonance to anchor into the art of self-creation. It's how I access *my* feminine frequency to make art I adore (and that others love, commission and buy), and design a life I genuinely love – where I write, travel, rest and reimagine, then re-create what's possible. I'm sharing it with you because this isn't theory. It's my lived and luscious practice.

Creating Art

When you align with the version of you who's already created the "thing", you stop creating from lack or doubt, and you start creating from memory. Yes, memory. Because if that version of you is entangled with you right now, then the art is already created in her world. She's written it. Painted it. You're now simply the vessel remembering it into being.

Designing Life

You're not building your dream life from a place that doesn't exist; you're syncing with the version of you who's already living it. Feel her frequency – the way she walks into rooms, makes decisions, tends her mornings – and then start living in harmony with her reality. This is embodied time travel, but please don't ask me to explain the science; ask me to share all the ways I've experienced it to be true: I have a gazillion stories.

Respelling Reality

Reality bends when you do, so when you believe a version of yourself is real, and you behave like she's in the room, the quantum field *will* respond. It's not magic or science – it's both, and working with the Moon and her phases will give you a rhythm as you attune and refine your thoughts, feelings and actions accordingly and reality shape-shifts to meet you.

Why Does Any of This Matter When the World's Burning?

It matters *because* the world's burning. It matters because the world *is* burning and we know that, like the Tower card, this time of transformation *is* creating necessary shifts and that is *not* always, rarely, ever, comfortable.

Look, if making art, dancing away your grief or resting in the dark feels "useless" right now, remember that's what they want you to believe.

What I know for certain is that we are magic. We are the OG creatrixes, source-resses and spell-casters, and if anyone knows how to bridge the space between What's Been Before and What Comes Next, it's us. We're the ones tasked with composting inherited stories and respelling new ones.

We are the edge-walkers, the ones who've said yes when they wanted us to say no and no when they wanted us to say yes. We're the ones who remember that healing isn't linear – it's lunar. It waxes and wanes. It descends before it ascends. It comes in spirals, not straight lines.

The good news? You don't need to be perfect or have anything figured out – you simply start where you are, because your body already knows the rhythm. You might have forgotten the song. And we are remembering it *all*, together.

We are the ones who can and will recreate, re-source and respell the terms of our existence and experience – our reality – from the inside out. We aren't here to fit in or fix systems that don't work, either; we're here to remember a *different* way. An ancient future, new and older, wiser way.

They want us to believe that nature and beauty don't matter. That storytelling, poetry, embodiment, and personal myth are insignificant. They want us to think that choosing ourselves is selfish. That feminine power is dangerous. (FYI, it is: dangerous to the structures that rely on our compliance.)

So yes, it matters.

MAKE ART. SPEAK YOUR TRUTH. START BEFORE YOU'RE READY. HONOUR YOUR RHYTHMS.

CREATE AND LIVE A LIFE SO FULL, SO JUICY AND SO CONTRADICTORY THAT YOU DISRUPT IT ALL.

Respelling reality is a radical and rebellious act of self-creation (and trust) in a world that constantly tries to hijack our truth, our magic and our creative power.

Do it for yourself.

Do it for each other.

Do it for OUR future selves.

Do it for the women who didn't and still don't have the chance.

Do it because we are ALL remembering and that remembering is contagious. This is how we respell *OUR* reality.

FURTHER READING

Bair, Deirdre, *Anaïs Nin: A Biography*, Bloomsbury, London, 1996

Blanchflower, Melissa, et al., *Faith Ringgold*, Verlag der Buchhandlung Walther Konig, Cologne, 2022

Butler, Octavia E, *Kindred*, Headline, London, 2018

———————, *Parable of the Sower*, Headline, London, 2019

Clark, Garth, *Gilded Vessel: The Lustrous Life and Art of Beatrice Wood*, North Light Books, London, 2001

Dalmia, Yashodhara, *Amrita Sher-Gil: A Life*, Penguin Books India, New Delhi, 2013

Dispenza, Joe, *Becoming Supernatural: How Common People Are Doing the Uncommon*, Hay House, Carlsbad, 2019

Freestone, Clare, ed., *Yevonde: Life and Colour,* National Portrait Gallery, London, 2023

George, Lynell, *A Handful of Earth, a Handful of Sky: The World of Octavia E. Butler,* Angel City Press, Santa Monica, 2020

Fuentes, Carlos, ed., *The Diary of Frida Kahlo: An Intimate Self-Portrait,* Abrams, New York, 2005

Herrera, Hayden, *Frida: A Biography of Frida Kahlo*, Bloomsbury, London, 2018

Johnston, Jill, Marella Caracciolo Chia, and Giulio Pietromarchi, *Niki de Saint Phalle and The Tarot Garden*, Benteli Verlag, Salenstein, 2010

Lindauer, Margaret A, *Devouring Frida: The Art History and Popular Celebrity of Frida Kahlo*, Wesleyan University Press, Middletown, 1999

Lister, Lisa, *Code Red: Know Your Flow, Unlock Your Super Powers and Create a Bloody Amazing Life. Period*, Hay House UK, London, 2020

——————, *Self Source-ery: Come to Your Senses. Trust Your Instincts. Remember Your Magic*, Hay House UK, London, 2022

——————, *The Red Journal: Track Your Periods, Sync with Your Cycle and Unlock Your Monthly Superpowers*, SHEbear Creative, 2025

Louvish, Simon, *Mae West: It Ain't No Sin*, Thomas Dunne Books, New York, 2006

McIntosh, Martin, and Gemma Jones, eds., *Night Flower: The Life & Art of Vali Myers*, Outré Gallery Press, Melbourne, 2013

Menichetti, Gianni, *Vali Myers: A Memoir*, Golda Foundation, Moraga, CA, 2006

Morineau, Camille, et al., eds., *Niki de Saint Phalle: Structures for Life*, MOMA, New York, 2021

Nin, Anaïs, *The Diary of Anaïs Nin (1931–1974)*, unabridged editions, Harcourt Brace Jovanovich, New York, 1980

Pritchett, Price, *The Quantum Leap Strategy*, Pritchett LP, 2006

Roberts, Pam, and Robin Gibson, *Madame Yevonde: Colour, Fantasy and Myth*, National Portrait Gallery, London, 1990

Rodgers, Brett, ed., *Madame Yevonde: Be Original or Die*, British Council Visual Arts Publications, London, 1999

Ringgold, Faith, *We Flew Over the Bridge: The Memoirs of Faith Ringgold*, Duke University Press, Durham, NC, 2005

—————— and Michele Wallace, *Faith Ringgold: Politics/Power*, Weiss, Berlin, 2022

Rudick, Nicole, *What Is Now Known Was Once Only Imagined: An (Auto) Biography of Niki de Saint Phalle*, Siglio, South Egremont, MA, 2022

Sher-Gil, Amrita, *Amrita Sher-Gil: A Self-Portrait in Letters and Writings*, ed. Vivan Sundaram, Tulika Books, New Delhi, 2018

Sriram, Meera, *Between Two Worlds: The Art and Life of Amrita Sher-Gil*, Penny Candy Books, Oklahoma City, 2021

Spinks, Tracy, *Vali Myers: Dream Within a Dream*, Yarra & Hunter Arts Press, 2024

Vachharajani, Anita, *Amrita Sher-Gil: Rebel with a Paintbrush*, Harper Collins India, Gurgaon, Haryana, 2018

Wallace, Marlene, and Beatrice Wood, *Playing Chess with the Heart: Beatrice Wood at 100*, Chronicle Books, San Francisco, 1994

West, Mae, *Goodness Had Nothing to Do With It*, Macfadden-Bartell, New York, 1970

Wood, Beatrice, *I Shock Myself: The Autobiography of Beatrice Wood*, Schiffer Publishing, Atglen, PA, 2018

BIG LOVE, ALL THE GRATITUDE AND RED LIPSTICK KISSES TO

• • •

The SHE POWER COLLECTIVE – women, thank you for living this book in real time with me. I love our online circle of source-ery studies SO MUCH and I'm FOREVER grateful that you trust me to hold space for us to navigate this time and place on Planet Earth, right now, together – what a time to be alive!

The Hot Viking, Rich Lister – your patience, bread-baking abilities, kisses, dance breaks, road trips and all the support, in all the ways, are just a few of the gazillion reasons why marrying you was the best decision I EVER made!

EVERYONE at Watkins, thank you for making the creation of this book such a gorgeous and glorious process! Special shouts to Fiona for commissioning the book, Sue for your amazing edits and Ella for supporting and trusting me!

My ride-or-dies: Leanne, Sarah, Nicolas, David, Karen, Katie and Louise – thank farrrrrrrrrrrk for you!

Every woman/human who's ever read/bought/shared any of my books, thank you for your support – emotionally, energetically and financially – thank you! We now get to respell reality – TOGETHER!